OPEN SOURCE SOFTWARE: COMPARING PRODUCTIVITY

BASSAM A. BOKHOWA

OPEN SOURCE SOFTWARE: COMPARING PRODUCTIVITY

BY

BASSAM A. BOKHOWA

A Thesis Submitted in Partial Fulfillment of the Requirement for the Degree of Master of Information Technology.

Open University Malaysia

Kingdom of Bahrain

2009

ISBN: 1448643228

EAN-13: 9781448643226

بسم الله الرحمن الرحيم

In the name of Allah,

Most Gracious, Most Merciful

ABSTRACT

"Open Source Software: Comparing Productivity"

By: Bassam Bokhowa
tobassam@gmail.com

A descriptive study quantifying the short-term effects on employee productivity when migrating software on their desktop computers to Open Source software alternatives for the work environment. Through survey and experimentation, research and observation, the study compares employee productivity changes in the case of proprietary to Open Source software migration for both the desktop computer's operating system and its application software. Localization issues for the Arabic region are an integral part of this study as well. The study mainly aims to design a re-usable productivity benchmarking method along with the necessary localized programmatic tools for performing the same study as and when necessary in the future. This may be performed upon products and technologies as they progress or whenever required by decision makers. This knowledge is intended to assist decision-makers of any organization - especially in the Arab region – in their evaluation of proprietary software models against Open Source alternatives from the "client computer" perspective. Such a study is especially important in the global economic downturn that had started since 2008. Recommendations are included at the end of the study.

Keywords: Bassam Bokhowa, Information Technology, IT, CIO, open source, free software, desktop applications, organization, employee, productivity, migration, Bahrain, Arab, Arabian Gulf, OpenOffice.org, Firefox, Linux, Ubuntu, Middle East, Thesis, VirtualBox, Windows Vista, Microsoft, Intaj.

DEDICATION

To the architect of change, in spite of those who fear it. To the

beloved prophet,

M u h a m m a d
peace and prayers upon him.

ACKNOWLEDGEMENTS

First and foremost, I – the researcher - acknowledge Him whom I could not have lifted a finger without; Thank you Allah, my Lord and Creator, for the mercy and care which have touched me in moments of dire need.

Then, I – the researcher - would like to heartily acknowledge:

- Abubakr Bassam Bokhowa, for programming skills rendered to the project

- Mr. Ahmad Kananah, and Mrs. Rola Yusif - lecturers at the Arab Open University - for their generous guidance and timely insight

- my colleagues, the staff, and the students at the Arab Open University - Bahrain Branch for their sincere cooperation with my experiment

I ask Allah that He bless you all, and guide you with His light.

TABLE OF CONTENTS

LIST OF TABLES

LIST OF FIGURES

CHAPTERS

Information Technology is to commerce in the twenty-first century what wind was to the Royal Navy in the eighteenth century, what coal was to the Industrial Revolution, what philosophy was to the Enlightenment, and what art was to the Renaissance – *Adam Kolawa, "How Better Software Can Save the World"*

1. INTRODUCTION

1.1 Background Information

Many organizations today rely heavily on computer technology placed on employees' desktops to aid their work productivity. The Gartner research firm estimates that there are a recorded 1.014 billion personal computer machines that have been shipped since their introduction in 1975 up until June 2002. Approximately 81.5 percent of PCs shipped have been desktops. Seventy-five percent of these machines have gone into professional, or work-related, environments. Gartner analyst Martin Reynolds wrote:

> *This demand exists because of the power of the PC to leverage intellectual capital, unlocking the capabilities of individuals to succeed and companies to profit. [...] However, expanding the market will require that PCs become smaller and even less expensive than they are today, while delivering greater functionality and performance (Kanellos, 2002).*

Desktop computer technology consists of hardware components as well as software programs. These are both part of the high expense dilemma that stops technology from permeating into many organizations and even whole countries.

The most installed software on desktop computers today is the Microsoft Windows line of operating systems (Net Applications, 2009) and the Microsoft Office suite of application software which had recorded a 95% market share figure in 2007 according to research firm International Data Corp (Knowledge@Wharton, 2007). Both software include important tools for browsing and communicating information on both local networks as well as the wider Internet network.

Microsoft – as other software development companies - charges a price for licensing the use of their software solutions by any individual, with varying plans for organization-wide licensing. Upgrades to newer versions of software are issued with new features, which entails that organizations may be constantly paying Microsoft for new upgrade licenses. This is especially true in the following situations:

1. Some newer versions of application software will output new document formats that are not natively readable by older versions of the same application software. Organizations that have upgraded to the most recent version of application software for need of newer features will be reason enough for related organizations to upgrade as well in order to be compatible with their client or vendor's document formats. Microsoft Office 2007 is an example of a newer application software version that introduces new document formats (Weir, 2007).

2. Newer versions of application software will at times require an upgrade of the operating system software in order to run. Microsoft Office 2007 – for example – will only run on the Microsoft Windows Xp version of the Windows operating system or later versions (Microsoft Corporation, 2009). This

will have a domino effect with Office upgrades tying-in with Windows upgrades as a prerequisite.

In another related development, a worldwide group-initiative existed in the 80s throughout the programming community, and was further fueled by the Internet communication revolution, in order to make software freely available to all individuals and organizations.

It resulted in a large and diverse variation of operating systems and application software for desktop computers under the common name of "Free Software" and later, "Open Source Software", or OSS, FOSS, and FLOSS (Stallman, 2008).

1.2 Research Problem

Microsoft Corporation has recently announced the phase-out of support for its previous desktop operating system software – Windows Xp – by mid-April 2009. Customers are faced with the Microsoft-proposed solution of migrating to the newer Microsoft Vista operating system (Microsoft Corporation, 2009).

The new Microsoft desktop operating system is not without issues of concern to Microsoft's customers. Some reasons for the hesitance to upgrade, shown by some, follow here:

(I)　The higher computer hardware requirements needed to run the Microsoft Vista operating system (Microsoft Corporation), which in turn add to the cost of the upgrade or leave organizations fearing lower productivity from slower performance on current desktop hardware that has not been upgraded. Everdream says 79.9% of business machines do not match Microsoft's recommended requirements for premium-ready PCs upgradeable to Windows Vista (ZDNet Research , 2007).

(II)　Radical changes in the Microsoft Vista operating system's presentation elements and security features - compared to the previous Microsoft desktop operating systems - translate into further user-training costs as well as compatibility issues with older application software, both of which could also potentially affect employee productivity (Berlind, 2007) as well as entailing a further domino effect of upgrades to their software.

Whether for these or other reasons, it has been noted that Microsoft Windows usage share has recently dropped below 90% for the first time in two years. The drop in the Windows Xp usage share has not been accompanied by an equal rise in the Windows Vista usage share either (Keizer, 2008).

Open Source software solutions are now being offered as an effective and cost-saving alternative to proprietary desktop operating systems and application software. Brendan Scott, an Australian lawyer specializing in IT and telecommunications law, studied TCO for both proprietary and Open Source software and stated:

> *Customers attempting to evaluate a free software v proprietary solution can confine their investigation to an evaluation of the ability of the packages to meet the customer's needs, and may presume that the long run TCO will favor the free software package. Further, because the licensing costs are additional dead weight costs, a customer ought to also prefer a free software solution with functionality shortfalls where those shortfalls can be overcome for less than the licensing cost for the proprietary solution. (Scott, 2002)*

This statement has been demonstrated by the model devised by Open Source solutions provider Cybersource (Cybersource® Pty. Ltd, 2004) and by the Linux server implementations studied by the Robert Frances Group (Robert Frances Group, Inc., 2002).

Yet, even though Open Source server solutions are successfully widespread (Smith, et al., 2003), many reasons have been cited for the slow adoption of FLOSS on desktop computers, mainly:

- Psychological negativity towards free alternatives (Dolezal, 2008)
- Lack of a clear "future roadmap" (Jackson, 2007)
- Full-circle file compatibility issues with proprietary software (Sylvester, 2008)
- Lack of tiered support (Swigart, et al., 2008)
- Need for data migration
- Lack of simplicity (Dotzler, 2005)
- Hardware compatibility (Nielson, 2008)
- Large number of diverse distributions (Gralla, 2007)

Recently, rapid developments in Open Source desktop software's usability, supportability, and hardware compatibility have led to many announcements from the Open Source community that their desktop software is now friendly enough for mainstream desktop computer users – especially in organizational environments - and not simply enthusiasts who are ready to go through complicated procedures in order to access commonly used features as before. Indeed, the growth in desktop usage of the Linux operating system has seen a record high in the year 2008 (see "Data from Market Share: Top Operating System Share Trend" on page 199). Latest estimates place Linux desktop users at no less than 8 million users (Dotzler, 2009), while some go as high as 29 million (The Linux Counter, 2009). The user base has certainly earned the client-side much organizational credibility in all cases, as will be discussed later in Chapter 2.

With the global economic downturn rearing its head in the year 2008, many decision-makers in diverse organizations are contemplating the advantages of Open Source desktop software as an alternative at this point. Still many fear that the impact of such a radical change on the overall productivity of their establishment's computing environment may outweigh any direct economical advantages.

1.3 Objectives of Study

This project aims to aid decision-makers at organizations evaluating a migration of desktop computer operating systems and application software to Open Source alternatives. It aims to do so through researching the effects on employee productivity that such a migration might have. This will mainly be done by comparing usage data of Open Source software with a baseline of employee performance while using proprietary software solutions. The project aims to utilize the following mechanism:

1. Research the most common organizational desktop software required globally and the available OSS alternatives to satisfy such requirements.
2. Verify previous findings of step 1 locally through an investigation using a survey questionnaire.
3. Research the most appropriate Open Source alternatives for results achieved previously in 'step 2' above.
4. Create proprietary and Open Source desktop software solutions incorporating the findings in steps 1 and 2 above.
5. Create an experiment utilizing a standard testing script for subjects to execute on both previous solutions with the means to measure user productivity during execution of the script instructions.
6. Create a programmatic benchmarking tool executable on the widest possible array of diverse platforms and localized to support the Arabic language.

1.4   Significance of Study

The significance of this study will be in uncovering and verifying decision-making information through research, experimentation, surveys, observation and interviews. This information may be critically important for concerned organizations and would lay significant light on the subject matter for strategists in both the organizational and technical fields. For example:

- This study offers a quantitative methodology for the calculation and comparison of employee productivity while using a desktop computer.
- The study aids decision-makers in making decisions that usually cost organizations a considerable amount of their budgets each year in terms of software licensing, maintenance, and support.
- The study also aims to create a re-usable benchmarking process and the necessary localized programmatic tools for performing the same study in the future, whether upon products and technologies as they progress or as and when needed by decision makers.
- The study uncovers the short-term effects on employee productivity when changing from their most-used operating system and application software.
- The study verifies the most common application software categories presently used in diverse organizations, both globally and at the local level in the Kingdom of Bahrain.
- The study attempts to touch on the subject of what psychological "employee response" to expect - in the short-

term - when migrating their desktop computers to Open Source software solutions.

1.5   Scope of Study

Open Source solutions: Of the available operating system and application software alternatives, this study restricts itself to selecting only from within the available Open Source solutions.

Desktop software: This study will also not involve the server solutions available from the Open Source software community and widely used in organizations worldwide, since many studies have covered different aspects of such solutions already. In contrasting with software, hardware is also not an issue discussed in this study. Therefore, hardware compatibility for users with needs for special hardware equipment are not part of this study's scope.

Organizational: The study also restricts its research of activities to organization-related ones and not the personal or entertainment needs of any individuals.

The home or personal computer user does not fall under the scope of this study because of the wide variety of software used by that user category. Today's Open Source software solutions either do not have a solution available to suffice the home user's every need or – for those that are available - do not match the user's taste or level of computer skill[1].

This study also excludes the activities of non-employees who use the technology infrastructure of an organization, such as students in educational establishments, as their productivity does not directly affect the organization's profitability. Hence, the study also excludes the kiosk systems tailored by some organizations for use by their customers.

Individuals therefore need to be involved in the use of desktop computer software in some form of organizational endeavor in order to count as part of this study's population. They should also be accountable for their productivity towards their organization's profitability in order to be considered.

Some non-governmental organizations (NGOs) are charities that have employees who are unpaid volunteers and are rarely accountable for their productivity. These individuals do not fall within the study population.

Productivity: Though there are many factors contributing to an organization's decision to adopt an Open Source strategy for their desktop software, this study will be restricted to measuring

---

[1] *"... while hackers can be very good at designing interfaces for other hackers, they tend to be poor at modeling the thought processes of the other 95% of the population well enough to write interfaces that J. Random End-User and his Aunt Tillie will pay to buy"* (Raymond, 2000).

only the employee productivity aspect. This entails actions directly contributing to an increase or decrease in the amount of organizational work done by an employee on a desktop computer in a limited span of time. No other effects, even though they may contribute indirectly to overall employee productivity in the workplace, are being measured in this study.

Short-term effects: This study will not be concerned with long-term effects on productivity, but only the short-term effects. This is because of the significant amount of resources needed and the lack of visible long-term Open Source organizational implementations on desktop computers in my country of residence; The Kingdom of Bahrain, where this study takes place.

1.6 Definition of Terms[2]

This is an alphabetical arrangement of words that are frequently used in the Open Source domain, and that are also used in several places in this thesis. Some words are familiar, but may have a slightly different meaning in this context. Italicized words are defined in their order within this list.

Application software: *software* used to achieve a specific practical function by *users* of a computer system.

Client computer: In *client/server architecture*, a client computer is the main computing tool used to request information and services from the *server computer*.

Client/server architecture: Network connectivity architecture whereby personal or individual computing devices called *client computers* are capable of requesting information and services through connectivity with other computing devices dedicated for serving these resources and called *server computers*.

Desktop computer: A stationary computing device (unlike a *laptop computer*) meant for personal or individual use (unlike a *server computer*), usually located on an office or home desk. A

---

2 Compiled from a number of web sources, namely:
http://www.techweb.com/encyclopedia ,
http://www.computeruser.com/resources/dictionary/ ,
http://www.webopedia.com/ , http://www.definethat.com/ .

desktop computer may also serve as the *client computer* in *client/server architecture*.

Desktop environment (Linux): A set of graphical *applications* built to seamlessly work together and enhance the usability of a *Linux operating system* to *users* through providing a user-friendly computing environment.

Desktop software: *Software* for personal or individual use on a *desktop computer*. This includes application software and the necessary *operating system* software needed as an environment to run such applications.

Distribution (Linux): Refers to the specific mix of software *packages* maintained under a published name with the common denominator of a *Linux* kernel component.

FOSS, or F/OSS: Free and Open Source Software, also referred to at times as FLOSS (Free/Libre and Open Source Software). "Libre" is used to distinguish the term 'free' as in the right to 'free speech' and not 'free' as in 'a gift' or 'at no cost'.

Free software: software that has been published under a license agreement that frees all persons to use it, distribute it, modify its *source code*, and publish the resulting product. Free here refers to a rightful freedom, ao in 'frcc speech'. This is the view is of the *Free Software Foundation*, see "Appendix A: The Free Software Definition" on page 159.

Free Software Foundation (FSF): founded by Richard Stallman - as part of the GNU project - on the belief that all software should be free, since all software development relies on previous knowledge, which is public domain, and therefore new knowledge - as a derivative - should also be free for all.

Freeware: software that has been published under a license agreement that frees persons and/or organizations to use it. Free here refers to 'no cost'. It is therefore a concept still based on the idea of copyright, with some articles waivered as a charity or gift. This view of software is opposed by the *Free Software Foundation* and they distance their own free software license by describing it as "Free, as in speech ...".

GNU: A project by the *Free Software Foundation* aimed at creating a completely free alternative to the Unix *operating system software*. GNU is a recursive acronym that stands for "Gnu is Not Unix".

Hardware: Physical components of a computer system including peripherals and storage devices.

Laptop computer: A mobile computing device (unlike a *desktop computer*) meant for personal or individual use (unlike a *server computer*). A laptop computer may also serve as the *client computer* in *client/server architecture*

Linux: *Operating system software* using *software components* (known as *packages*) from the *GNU* project - as well as other *open source* projects - and a kernel *software* component first devised by Linus Torvalds. Based on the components used, there are many Linux variations (*known as distributions*). Linux is also referred to by some as the GNU/Linux operating system.

Open Source movement: Though a branch (fork) of the Free Software movement, the open source movement believes that open source software should be a business choice, hence only appropriate when it makes business sense.

Open Source software: Essentially the same concept as *free software*. The difference comes from the delicate contrast in principle between the *Free Software Foundation* and the *Open Source Movement*. The term was developed to represent free software while emphasizing the 'freedom of use' aspect of the software (source code being open), and not allowing people to assume that 'free' meant 'at no cost'. Based on this, an open source derivative could be marketed for a cost under this scheme. See "Appendix B: The Open Source Definition (Annotated)" on page 164.

Operating system software: *software* that creates the necessary environment with the essential services – including interaction with computer *hardware* - that other software needs in order to execute their functions.

OSS: see *Open Source Software*.

Package (Linux): a software component that has one or more maintainers and used as a component in a *Linux distribution*.

Programming language: *Software* used to create other *software*.

Server computer: In *client/server architecture*, a server computer is the main repository for a set of information and services. The server accepts *client computer* requests for its resources and processes these requests according to predetermined authorization levels.

Software: *Programming language* code that serves a purpose, whether as an *operating system, application*, or to create another *programming language*.

Source code: The lines of *programming language* code used to create *software*.

User: End-user of a computer system. Mostly concerned with using a computer system's application software as a means to achieve a specific practical aim.

Virtualization software: *Software* that emulates in detail the working specifications of a computer's *hardware* in order to be able to run one *operating system* within the execution state of another.

2. LITERATURE REVIEW

2.1 History of Free Software and the Open Source Movement

2.1.1 Hacker Community

After the end of World War II, programmers were the dominant technical culture in computing. These programmers formed a culture, whose name 'hackers' first appeared in the early 1960s in the Massachusetts Institute of Technology. They "proudly call themselves hackers - not as the term is now abused by journalists to mean a computer criminal, but in its true and original sense of an enthusiast, an artist, a tinkerer, a problem solver, an expert" (Raymond, 1998). MIT was one of the main connection points for the first transcontinental high-speed computer network in built in 1969; ARPANET. The ARPANET had a profound effect in spreading the influence of the hacker culture (Williams, 2002).

That same year, an invention started that was to become home to the next generation of hackers; Unix. Unix is a very portable operating system invented by Ken Thompson and Denis Ritchie at Bell Labs. Because Unix contained built-in networking software (UUCP), it rapidly built its own networked culture. By 1980, Unix had spread to a large number of university and research sites, and Unix-based broadcast networks (Usenet) were rapidly growing faster than ARPANET (Rosenberg, 2000).

2.1.2 Free Software

Richard Stallman, a software engineer working at MIT, was frustrated when software companies began to restrict access to the source code of their software. and decided to take action. Stallman wanted to preserve what he believed is a natural human right: freedoms that accompany any piece of free software, which he specified as:

- Freedom 0: The freedom to run the program, for any purpose.
- Freedom 1: The freedom to study how the program works, and adapt it to your needs (access to the source code is a precondition for this freedom).
- Freedom 2: The freedom to redistribute copies so you can help your neighbor.
- Freedom 3: The freedom to improve the program, and release your improvements to the public, so that the whole community benefits (Stallman, 2008).

Stallman started building a Unix clone in 1982, under his 'GNU' project. The recursive acronym (GNU is Not Unix) was a hacker tradition (Stallman, 1998).

In order to prevent the misuse of these software, a legal structure was required. Stallman wrote the General Public License (GPL) to achieve this goal. The GPL is a smart hack to use the traditional copyright law to serve an opposite purpose. This method was called "copyleft" (Stallman, 1999).

An operating system is usually composed of several components: kernel, text editors, compilers, etc.. In September 1984, Stallman started the development of the EMACS text editor. Stallman intended to develop a kernel for the GNU operating system which was to be named after his sweetheart at the time: Alix. However, it was agreed that 'Hurd' would be a more suitable name.

By 1985, the GNU Project was growing, with many people participating and developing free software. The growth required funding in order to keep the momentum and Richard Stallman decided to establish the Free Software Foundation as a tax-exempt charity (Stallman, 2008).

In the meantime, the microcomputer revolution brought cheap computing power to the masses. It also attracted some Unix hackers to establish Sun Microsystems, a company aimed at providing Unix users on VAX minicomputers with individual workstation solutions built on Motorola 68000-based hardware and Ethernet networking (Raymond, 2000).

2.1.3   Linux Kernel

In 1987, and with the invention of the Intel 386 CPU, personal computer performance was beginning to compare with workstations. Hackers wanted to have an operating system for it that would provide the needed programming tools and had modifiable and redistributable source code. Commercial Unix was too expensive for this purpose though.

In 1990, Richard Stallman's Free Software Foundation had supplied almost all the other difficult parts of a Unix-like operating system through the GNU project, except for the operating system kernel. Multiple efforts had started to port or clone a Unix kernel to Intel 386 machines by 1991. Linus Torvalds, a Helsinki University student, led one of these efforts. Linus had found the DOS operating system inadequate and UNIX was too expensive for his Intel 386 machine. He succeeded in using the Free Software Foundation's GNU toolkit to develop a kernel modeled after the free educational Minix operating system and which followed the UNIX philosophy. Linus released the source code for his very simple kernel under the GPL and called it 'Linux'. Shortly after, many developers showed interest in the newborn kernel and started contributing to its development. Eric Raymond describes the development:

The most important feature of Linux, however, was not technical but sociological. Until the Linux development, everyone believed that any software as complex as an operating system had to be developed in a carefully coordinated way by a relatively small, tightly-knit group of people [...]. Linux evolved in a completely different way. From nearly the beginning, it was rather casually hacked on by huge numbers of volunteers coordinating only through the Internet. Quality was maintained not by rigid standards or autocracy but by the naively simple strategy of releasing every week and getting feedback from hundreds of users within days, creating a sort of rapid Darwinian selection on the mutations introduced by developers. To the amazement of almost everyone, this worked quite well.

The FSF decided to adopt Linux as the kernel of the GNU operating system, and called it GNU/Linux. Hacker efforts by the late 1990s had become centered upon Linux (Raymond, 2000).

2.1.4 Open Source Movement

The semantic confusion implicit in the use of the term "Free" scared businesses and software companies, as they believed it meant "at no cost". This was a hindrance to the growth and potential of Free Software.

In January 1998, Netscape announced a decision to release the source code of its web browser to the Internet as a part of its struggle against fierce competition from Microsoft. Seizing the opportunity to re-evangelize the philosophies of the hacker culture, Eric Raymond helped the Netscape team market the new strategy under the re-branded name for Free Software: 'Open Source'. Building on its success, they used Linux as the demonstration case and practical argument. The new strategy aimed at using guerrilla-marketing tactics towards the media serving Fortune 500 companies in order to get market 'buy-in' from the top down, with the promise of software with higher reliability, lower cost, and better features.

The facts on the ground at the time helped the Open Source movement immensely. Apache Open Source software and its derivatives were running fully 50% of the world's publicly accessible Web servers. Perl was the dominant programming language for the new breed of web-based applications. Sendmail routed more than 80% of all Internet email messages. Even the ubiquitous domain name system still depends almost entirely on an Open Source program called BIND.

The whole public-relations effort was master-minded by Eric Raymond in February of 1998, based on his perception of negative messages inadvertently sent by the Free Software Foundation or negative stereotyping that had surrounded the FSF in the minds of the trade press and the corporate world (e.g. "free" as in no cost, hostility to intellectual property rights, communism, and others). Linus Torvalds endorsed the idea and within days, the Open Source Initiative (OSI) was born.

The OSI is based on a bill of rights for computer users called the Open Source Definition (see Appendix B: The Open Source Definition (Annotated) on page 164). OSI reviews different licenses for compliance with the OSD, and - if compliant - the licenses will be approved as Open Source licenses. As of the 18th of September 2006, the OSI had approved 62 licenses.

The distinction between Free Software and Open Source Software should be clearly noted. Free Software is any software that is distributed under the GNU General Public License (GPL). Open Source is any software that is distributed under any of the licenses approved by the OSI, including the GPL. The Open Source initiative allows more flexibility in defining the licensing terms.

By the early part of 1999 a trend began among big independent software vendors (ISVs) to port their business applications to Linux. Preliminary results from an August 1999 survey of 2000 IT managers revealed that 49% considered Linux an "important or essential" element of their enterprise computing strategies. In another survey - by IDC - 13% of the respondents had already employed Linux in business operations (Raymond, 2000).

2.1.5 Beyond Software

Though the Free Software movement centered its principles on the implications of free versus proprietary software licensing models, the Open Source movement – in contrast - started by highlighting the unique hacker development model behind free software, which Eric Raymond summarizes as that of "peer review, decentralization, and openness" (Raymond, 1998). He also describes the broader effect of such a model on society in general saying:

> The success of open source does call into some question the utility of command-and-control systems, of secrecy, of centralization, and of certain kinds of intellectual property. It would be almost disingenuous not to admit that it suggests (or at least harmonizes well with) a broadly libertarian view of the proper relationship between individuals and institutions (Raymond, 2002).

This model's social and economic implications were later taken into further detail by many authors in the Open Source community (Cooper, et al., 2006).

2.2 Organizational Adoption of Open Source Desktop Software

Following are a number of prominent examples of Open Source Software adoptions on desktop computers – as per the scope of this thesis described on page 27. These examples revolve around the use of complete Open Source Software solutions in the internal processes of both the public and private sectors. The mentioned cases are alphabetically ordered according to the related country's name.

2.2.1 Belgium

About half of the 12,891 desktop PCs in use at the Belgian Ministry of Justice are now running GNU/Linux and OpenOffice. The ministry decided in 2005 to install OpenOffice and the Suse GNU/Linux distribution on all new PCs. Minister Onkelinx had based her decision to migrate to an Open Source desktop on recommendations from the national government to use Open Standards. The ministry's goal is to make the GNU/Linux desktop its default. However, this will take some time, predicts the spokesperson for the ministry. "For starters, there are several peripherals, such as printers, that are incompatible with GNU/Linux. Next are a number of applications, some written in-house and some proprietary, that can not be used on GNU/Linux" (Hillenius, 2008).

2.2.2 Cuba

The Cuban government is to migrate thousands of its computers to open source software, in a move that distances the communist nation from US-based Microsoft.

Several Cuban government ministers backed the move at a technology conference. Communications minister Ramiro Valdes gave a pro-open source opening keynote, while Richard Stallman, head of the Free Software Foundation, told the conference proprietary software is inherently insecure.

A Cuban academic, Hector Rodriguez, is supporting the migration to open source by heading up a development programme within one of the largest Cuban universities. Cuba's customs service has already migrated to Linux, while the ministries of culture, higher education and communications are planning to do so, Rodriguez told the conference (Thurston, 2007).

2.2.3 Ecuador

On April 10, 2008, President Rafael Correa Delgado has signed Decree 1014 by ordering with absolute precision that the software used by public administrations in the country is free software (and implicitly based on opon standards) (Flui., 2008).

2.2.4 France

In 2001 the Gendarmerie Nationale, France's national police force, started introducing open source software. The main goals were to gain greater independence and flexibility than proprietary software could offer. The decision to migrate all new workstations to Ubuntu, taken in January 2008, was the most important step in this transition so far. About 5000 workstations have already been migrated and the target for December 2009 is 15,000 workstations. All 90,000 workstations are to be migrated by 2015 (Bierhals, 2009).

The 577 French members of parliament and their assistants started using the Ubuntu GNU/Linux distribution, beginning summer 2008. The parliament migration included 1145 PCs. The migration cost about 80,000 Euros. The French National Assembly decided to switch to an Open Source desktop in November 2007. The move was initiated by deputies Richard Cazenave and Bernard Carayon.

PSA Peugeot Citroën, Europe's second-largest car manufacturer has migrated to Suse Linux on 20,000 desktops. Novell announced the deal to deploy GNU/Linux as the biggest single company desktop Linux migration so far (Open Source Observatory and Repository, 2008).

2.2.5 Germany

The city of Munich had started one of the most thoroughly studied migration plans in 2001, and started actual migration gradually in 2006. Currently 1,400 out of the 14,000 intended desktop computers have been migrated to the custom-built LiMux distribution. In addition, 12,000 workstations have OpenOffice.org 2 installed on Windows and more than 100%

have Mozilla Firefox 1.5 and Mozilla Thunderbird 1.5 installed on Windows clients. The project aims to complete the migration by the end of 2011 (Municipality of Munich, 2008). Some argue that such a project with a budget of 35 million Euros and with the previous results in such a lengthy implementation time should be considered a failure (Munich Linux Watch, 2009). Nevertheless, the battle for Munich's Desktop proved the personal computer's importance as the last Microsoft bastion of business (Acohido, 2003).

The Foreign Ministry is also migrating all of its 11.000 desktops to GNU/Linux and other open source applications. The ministry has so far migrated almost four thousand of its desktops to GNU/Linux and expects to complete the move by the summer of 2009 (Hillenius, 2009).

2.2.6 India

The Tamil Nadu government has identified free and open-source software as a major strategic component in its efforts to build an inclusive information society. More than 3,000 Suse Linux desktops have been dispatched to government offices in Tamil Nadu (Tan, 2007).

2.2.7 Malaysia

Based on the decision by the cabinet of the Government of Malaysia, the Malaysian Public Sector OSS Master Plan was launched on 16 July 2004 to create and enhance value using OSS within the Public Sector ICT framework. The plan completed Phase I – OSS awareness, and entered Phase II – Accelerated Adoption – on 12th June 2007 targeting A full eco-system to allow natural growth of demand and supply in OSS in order to move forward to Phase III - Self Reliance - in the near future. On the desktop side, 491 computers have been migrated to Open Source solutions in the public sector's administrative offices to date (Malaysian Public Sector OSS Portal , 2009).

2.2.8   Netherlands

The Dutch government has published its cabinet policy in regards to OSS in an initiative to support the use of Open Source Software and Open Standards in the Netherlands. According to the published policy, all government departments and institutions in the public and semi-public sectors must introduce the "comply or explain, and commit" principle for ICT orders (purchase and tender) from 2 April 2008 (Central Government) or 31 December 2008 (subsidiary government bodies and other departments) for the application of open standards to new systems, modifications or contract extension (Ministry of Economic Affairs, 2007).

The Netherlands Patent Office and the Netherlands Competition Authority are the first of the countries national government bodies switching to an Open Source desktop (Open Source Observatory and Repository, 2008).

2.2.9   South Africa

At a Cabinet media briefing in South Africa, the government committed to open source implementation within its departments.

It also delivered several other statements concerning ICT. The government said it had approved a policy and strategy for open source implementation. It added that all new software developed for, or by government, will be based on open standards, and government will migrate current software to open source. "This strategy will, among other things, lower administration costs and enhance local IT skills," said the Cabinet statement. Cabinet spokesman Themba Maseko said, in reply to a question, that the process would probably be a lengthy one. He noted that a project office would be set up by April, by the Department of Science and Technology, with the Council for Scientific and Industrial Research, and the State IT Agency. The Cabinet statement said all major IT vendors in the country have supported the initiative and made contributions to the development of open source (GITOC, 2007).

2.2.10 Spain

The public government of the Spanish region of Extremadura has now a long tradition of promoting and using free software. 14,000 desktop computers in the public administration offices have been migrated from Microsoft Windows to their custom Linux distribution; gnuLinex (Calbet, 2005).

2.2.11 Switzerland

The administration of the Swiss canton Solothurn is migrating 2000 desktops to Open Source. The switch should be completed at the end of the year 2008, reports Kurt Bader, responsible for IT at the canton in the northwest of Switzerland. Bader presented on the migration project on the "Open Source Meets Business" conference that took place last month in Nürnberg. The biggest Open Source project in Switzerland is going "without issues, the changeover is a resounding success and a step forward", Bader is quoted in a news item on the Linux Kommunale website. Staff workers can access some applications that only run on Microsoft Windows, which are hosted on a central server. In the third phase of the migration project, these Windows-only applications will be replaced by software that is able to run on more than one operating system, explained Bader (Observatory, 2008).

2.2.12 Turkey

Among the most prolific user of Linux is the Ministry of Defense of Turkey, which uses about 4500 thin clients at its headquarters. The military Recruitment Division, part of the Ministry of Defence, announced switching to Linux on all of its desktops. Ankara Police Department has about 400 PCs running on Linux.

The Radio and Television Regulatory Authority (RTÜK) of Turkey uses over 100 Linux workstations on its digital archiving and retrieval system.

Manisa Province Health Directorate in western Turkey, has deployed over four hundred PCs running Linux throughout the province. Another health sector, Bursa Pharmacies' Coop, has one hundred and fifty PCs deployed throughout Turkey's western province running Linux.

The Petrol İş Workers Union in Turkey has about one hundred PCs running on Linux at its headquarters and 13 branch offices round the country.

Neziroglu Motors has about one hundred PCs running on Linux at its headquarters and 5 branch offices (Sowe, 2008).

2.2.13 United States of America

Novell migrated 5000 employee desktops to their Suse Enterprise Desktop product after measuring the business value and ROI (Novell Inc., 2004).

2.2.14 Venezuela

The Venezuelan government in 2005 passed "Directive 3.390", a law that requires the entire government to migrate to open source before December 2007. In 2002, the traditional, social elite-backed administrators of PDVSA (Venezuela's state-owned oil company) decided that they didn't agree with President Chávez's policy decisions, which included re-directing profits from the oil company elites into social programs (including literacy and medical programs). These administrators were so adamant about their position, they illegally shut down the oil company, locked out the workers, and took control over the software that ran the corporation Conveniently, that software had been contracted to a US company called SAIC, which has well-known relationships with the US Department of Defense and CIA. In response to the illegal lock-out and sabotage of oil production in Venezuela, federal authorities were sent to

PDVSA's headquarters to reclaim the facility. The SAIC workers fled the country — after they had changed all the passwords that ran PDVSA's computer systems and set themselves up with remote control of these systems. Since the software was proprietary, no one except the SAIC workers knew how the software worked internally and the oil facilities were literally held hostage by criminals who were now seeking refuge in the United States. Why US authorities did not take action and apprehend these criminals is up for the reader's interpretation. If the SAIC workers had used their remote access to destroy the data, they would have effectively sabotaged oil production in Venezuela for months, if not years.

The Venezuelan government recruited some computer security experts who were able to reverse engineer SAIC's software, cut off their remote control of the computer systems and return access to the legal administrators of PDVSA. After this startling information warfare scenario had played out in real life, threatening the entire economy of a sovereign state by a multinational software firm with strong ties to a foreign defense and intelligence agency, President Chávez fully embraced open source, free software and mandated that all government systems be migrated to this more secure solution (northxsouth, 2008).

In August 2008 the IT agency CNTI said that nearly 60% of Venezuela's government offices had switched from proprietary software to open source, compared with its target of 100% migration by yearend 2008. Some ministries stood out for their progress. Venezuela's Social Development Ministry had reportedly already migrated 93% of its PCs and all of its servers to open source, having started the migration in 2007 (Venezuela Information Technology Report Q1 2009, 2009).

2.2.15 Vietnam

Minister of Information and Communications Le Doan Hop asked that by June 30, 2009, 100% of clients of IT divisions of government agencies must be installed with open source software; 100% of staffs at these IT divisions must be trained in the use of these software products and at least 50% use them proficiently.

IT divisions at government agencies comprise the IT departments of ministries and government agencies, provincial and municipal Departments of Information and Communications.

 Open source software products are OpenOffice, email software for servers of Mozilla ThunderBird, Mozilla FireFox web browser, and the Vietnamese typing software Unikey.

The instruction also said that by December 31, 2009, 70% of clients of ministerial agencies and local state agencies must be installed with the above open source software products and 70% of IT staff trained in using this software; and at least 40% able to use the software in their work

The above agencies were requested to increase the number of documents and information exchanged among them processed by the above software. By December 31, 2010, all staff at these agencies must be able to use open source software in their jobs.

The instruction also requests that computer traders not sell PCs installed with cracked software, but open source ones (VietNamNet.vn, 2009).

2.3   Measuring Employee's Software Productivity

2.3.1   Determining Employee Productivity

Productivity is a ratio relating output to one or more of the inputs associated with producing that output. While there is no disagreement on this general notion, a look at the productivity literature and its various applications reveals very quickly that there is neither a unique purpose for, nor a single measure of, productivity (Schreyer, 2001).

Output is the goods and services an organization delivers, which return revenue. Input is the cost of capital and labor required to produce the goods and services. The most common productivity measure is labor productivity, which relates output to employment or labor hours. An increase in output per unit of input is an increase in productivity. To increase productivity, therefore, an organization can increase output, decrease input, or perform both (U.S. Bureau of Labor Statistics).

2.3.2   Measuring Employee Productivity

We can measure employee productivity through attributes of task performance such as speed and accuracy of task completion, ease of learning, memorability of work procedures, and job satisfaction, as described by Intel in Figure 1. Employee Productivity Measures on page Error! Bookmark not defined.. Therefore, in order to improve employee productivity, we need gains in per-employee efficiencies or effectiveness — in essence, accomplishing more in less time (Intel Corporation,

2003). This is also the approach defined by SAP User Productivity department for gauging user productivity (Gillar, 2004).

We can measure many tangible areas of productivity in a straightforward manner. Other areas however, including office employee productivity, are less tangible, and therefore harder to measure in some work settings, see page 64.

2.3.3 Oracle's KLM Methodology

Oracle utilizes a methodology called Keystroke Level Modeling (KLM) which was created more than 20 years ago by researchers at Carnegie Mellon University and Xerox PARC. With KLM, each user action is assigned a standard time. For example, clicking on a button with a mouse takes 230 milliseconds, and moving your hand from the mouse to the keyboard takes 360 milliseconds. There also are standard times for mental operations. For example, locating the right icon in a toolbar takes 1350 milliseconds. The times for many activities have been standardized by taking the average time from trials from many experienced users. Furthermore, times for new activities can be standardized in the same way.

With KLM, the estimated time to complete a task can be obtained by determining every step needed to complete it successfully and then adding up the standard times for all of the steps. The total should be an estimate of the time it will take an experienced user to complete the task.

While there have been dozens of published studies showing that KLM can predict time within 10%-30% of actual user time, there are few examples of its usage in the fast-pace nature of commercial software development.

KLM findings are usually supported through comparing results with observed lab-environment testing of an application's actual impact on a small sample of experiment subjects (Sauro, et al., 2008).

2.3.4 Intel's Employee Productivity Measurement Methodology (EPMM)

In 2001, the IT Business Value (ITBV) team at Intel developed a methodology to measure changes that occur when technology tools are introduced into an environment. The methodology combines sophisticated data collection methods, carefully monitored studies, and statistical data analysis to gauge the business value of new IT products and processes. According to Intel, this methodology has proven particularly useful in conducting experimental or field studies measuring employee productivity.

Intel previously measured the success of an IT tool in an organization by measuring higher availability, uptime, and number of trouble calls answered for it. That methodology, however, did not show Intel the impact of that tool on Intel's "bottom line". The new methodology evaluates a set of 20 or so metrics, called "value dials" that measure the changes that occur when new tools are introduced into an environment.

Figure 1: Intel's Employee Productivity Measures

Category	Measurement	How to Achieve It
Efficiency	• Amount of the user takes to complete a task • Number of tasks, or proportion of a large task, of various kinds that can be completed within a given time limit • Ratio between tasks that were completed versus not completed • Amount of dead time when the user is not interacting with the system	• Reduce the time it takes to perform a task • Restructure the nature of the tasks
Accuracy	• Ratio between tasks that were successful versus those that resulted in errors • Amount of time spent recovering from errors • Number of user errors	• Remove or reduce errors • Reduce the number of end-user processes to achieve the same goal, lowering the probability of errors • Reduce the costs associated with making an error • Remove a task that a person performs
Ease of Learning	• Number of features used versus not used by the users • Number of features that a user can remember or recall • Frequency of use of job aids such as user manuals or user help wizards • Amount of time taken by the user to achieve an acceptable level of performance • How frequently the manual or help tool solved the user problem	• Design product so that it reduces testing time • Provide adequate training materials and help tools
Satisfaction	• Number of times the user expresses frustration in completing the task • Number of times the user has to work around a difficult work procedure	• Improve the overall user experience

The changes measured will depend on a framework that takes the following aspects into account:

1. Studying the context of work to be measured
2. Knowledge of the available variables to be measured within the context

Figure 2: Phases of Intel's Employee Productivity Measurement Methodology (EPMM)

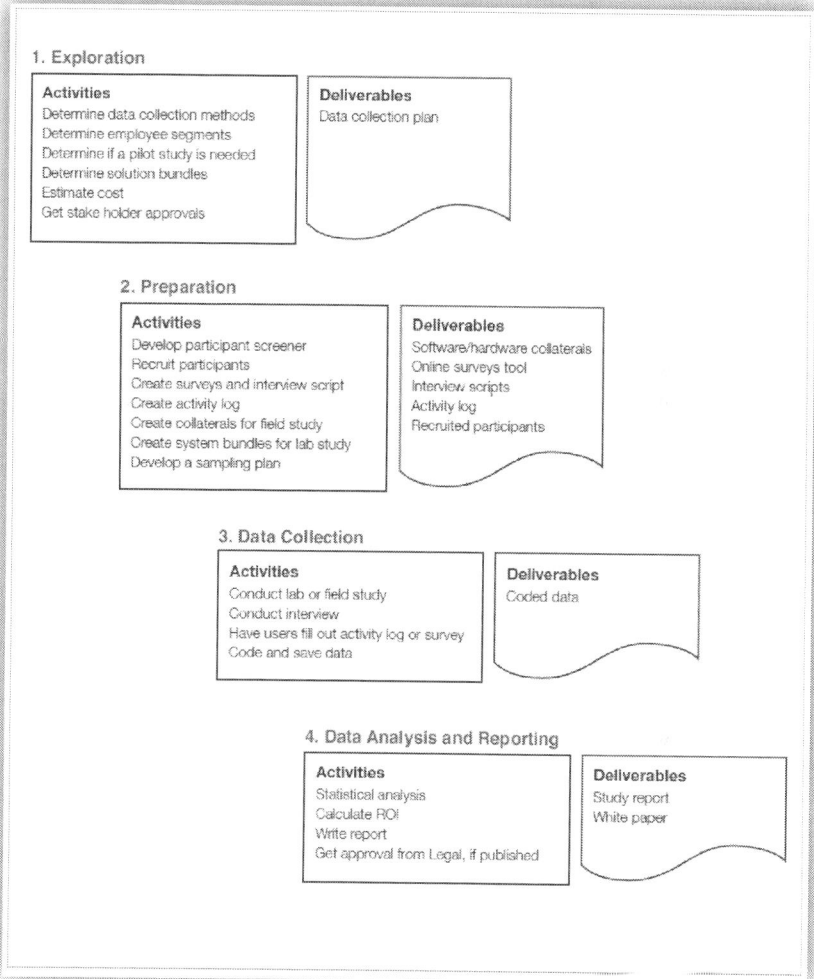

1. Exploration

Activities
Determine data collection methods
Determine employee segments
Determine if a pilot study is needed
Determine solution bundles
Estimate cost
Get stake holder approvals

Deliverables
Data collection plan

2. Preparation

Activities
Develop participant screener
Recruit participants
Create surveys and interview script
Create activity log
Create collaterals for field study
Create system bundles for lab study
Develop a sampling plan

Deliverables
Software/hardware collaterals
Online surveys tool
Interview scripts
Activity log
Recruited participants

3. Data Collection

Activities
Conduct lab or field study
Conduct interview
Have users fill out activity log or survey
Code and save data

Deliverables
Coded data

4. Data Analysis and Reporting

Activities
Statistical analysis
Calculate ROI
Write report
Get approval from Legal, if published

Deliverables
Study report
White paper

3. The timeframe, in which a baseline measurement will be taken

The following basic elements, for example, can capture employee productivity in most settings:

- Reduce the time it takes to complete an activity

- Reduce or remove user errors
- Reduce time needed to gain proficiency in an activity
- Remove the activity a user performs
- Restructure the nature of the activities to eliminate all or a portion of the activities

The EPMM is an essential component of the new methodology that utilizes a rigorous four-phase investigation approach, as summarized in Figure 2: Phases of Intel's Employee Productivity Measurement Methodology. The EPMM is also briefly detailed here as this project will utilize the methodology within its experiments.

2.3.4.1 Phase 1: Exploration

There are numerous data collection methods that can be utilized by this methodology, as can be seen in Figure 3: Data Collection Methods in Intel's Methodology. This phase will decide which of these methods is most appropriate for the variables to be studied and will result in a detailed data collection plan. The plan consists of the following points:

• Study scope and objectives

• Types of data collection techniques

• Time frames

• Study design

• Employee segments

• Sampling plan

- Product features or vectors for testing

- Use of probable tasks or scenarios, or both

- Participant recruitment process

- Required team members

- Possible study locations.

Figure 3: Data Collection Methods in Intel's Methodology

Method	Description	Best for Collecting...	Advantages	Disadvantages
Interview	Employees answer a series of semi-structured questions posed by an interviewer.	Qualitative employee feedback	Excellent method for collecting employee feed-back on the employee's likes and dislikes.	Rarely used for collecting employee performance data, such as task completion time and frequency. Asynchronous self-reporting data on task completion time and frequency are subject to reporting bias, which can result in over- or under-estimation.
Survey	Employees answer a series of structured questions.	Qualitative employee feedback	Easy to administer and is conducted on a large number of employees.	Asynchronous self-report data on task completion time and frequency are subject to reporting bias, which can result in over- or under-estimation. Often overused due to ease of administration.
User Activity Log	Employees answer a series of questions on the tasks that they performed that day or week.	Quantitative performance data	Easy to administer to a large population to obtain quantitative data on a regular basis.	Asking users to complete activity log just after performing the task could interfere with the work process.
Server Activity Log	The network or application server is queried for data such as frequency and duration of application usage.	Quantitative performance data	Very ease to query and obtain the data from the server on user activity.	Adequate configuration of the server infrastructure is required to obtain the data log. Possible to miss the context in which the event happened and the goal of the user.
Field Study	Employees are observed performing a series of tasks in their work environment.	Qualitative and quantitative performance data, depending on method used	Used for obtaining quantitative perform-ance data on low structure data that are difficult to simulate in the lab.	No control over the task and environment variables. Confounding variables can make the data less valid.
Lab Study	Employees perform a series of tasks in the lab environment.	Quantitative performance data	Best for collecting task performance data. Better control of task and environment variables.	Can only measure tasks that can be reproduced in the lab. Preparatory work and collateral needed. Artificial nature of the lab setting.

The plan also outlines project tasks, dependencies, durations, start and end dates, resources required, and cost estimates.

2.3.4.2 *Phase 2: Preparation*

In the preparation phase, all the collateral needed must be gathered — the appropriate hardware and software, along with any documents that participants will use during the study. This phase will also prepare scripts, any survey tools, activity logs, and a list of study participants.

2.3.4.3 *Phase 3: Data Collection*

This is the main data collection phase for the data to be later analyzed. Data collection is done through interviews, surveys, activity logs, field studies, and lab studies.

Interviews determine what helps or hinders participants in accomplishing their tasks. Surveys help identify the tasks we want to measure. Activity logs work well for collecting information on task frequency. In this phase data may also be gathered through setting up lab studies as detailed on page 61. Data collected in the lab helps ensure that the only variable impacting participant performance is the solution, and that other factors are controlled when the participants are completing their tasks.

2.3.4.4 *Phase 4: Data Analysis and ROI Generation*

The goal of this phase is to produce a final report compiling qualitative and quantitative data gathered and its analysis.

Top issues and comments are compiled along with the participant's level of satisfaction with the system bundle. Data from interviews, surveys, and activity logs is analyzed in order to provide an understanding of the participant's positive and negative comments.

Figure 4: Steps For Creating A Test System at Intel Labs

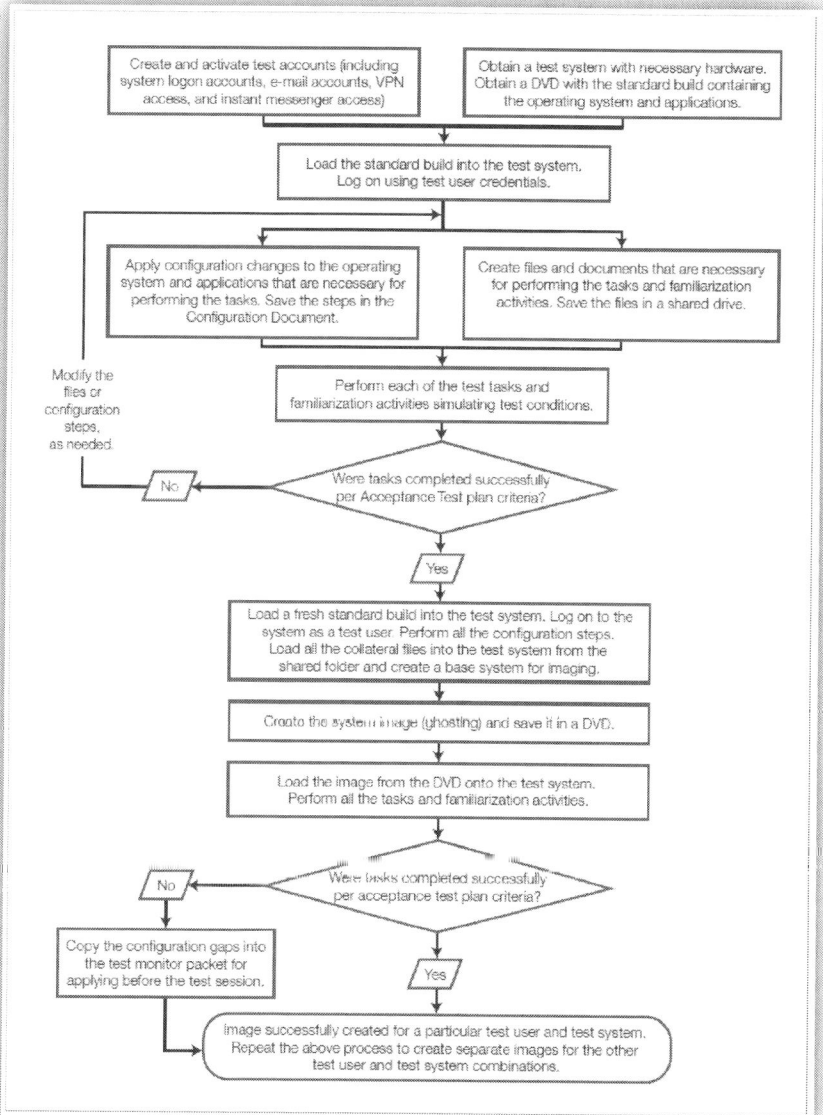

The activity log, field studies, and lab studies provide task completion data. Data obtained is coded and compiled in a spreadsheet. To evaluate the differences between conditions, standard statistical tests such as a t-test or an analysis of variance (ANOVA) are performed, using standard statistical software packages. A t-test assesses whether the means of two groups are statistically different from each other. This analysis is appropriate whenever we want to compare the means of two groups, and especially appropriate as the analysis for the posttest-only two-group randomized experimental design (Trochim, 2006), as is the case in Intel's methodology. The formula for the t-test is

$$t = \frac{\bar{X}_T - \bar{X}_C}{\sqrt{\frac{var_T}{n_T} + \frac{var_C}{n_C}}}$$

The *paired-samples T test* is a comparison test specially designed to compare values from the same group at different times. The values could be gathered before and after an event, or before and after a passage of time (Griffith, 2007).

Although a specific minimum p-value is not set, a result of 0.05 or below is typically considered as significant.

Calculations are summarized in Figure 5: Calculating Time Savings in Intel's Methodology, where the employee productivity benefit to the company is calculated in dollars per year as follows: **Employee Productivity Benefit** = Y * N*W* { Σ (Ta– Tb

) * F } Where: **Y** = Number of work weeks in a year, typically 49, **N** = Total number of employees in a company, **W** = Average wage rate or the burden rate for an employee, in dollars per hour, **Ta** = Average time taken to complete a task in the new system bundle in hours, **Tb** = Average time taken to complete a task in the baseline bundle in hours, **F** = Average frequency of the task performance for that task per week (Intel Corporation, 2004).

Figure 5: Calculating Time Savings in Intel's Methodology

Task Number	Average task completion time in the baseline system bundle (T_a)	Average task completion time in the final system bundle (T_b)	Difference $(T_a - T_b)$	Frequency of task performance per week (F)	Total time difference per week $(T_a - T_b) \times F$
Task 1	T_{1a}	T_{1b}	$(T_{1a} - T_{1b})$	F_1	$(T_{1a} - T_{1b}) * F_1$
Task 2	T_{2a}	T_{2b}	$(T_{2a} - T_{2a})$	F_2	$(T_{2a} - T_{2b}) * F_2$
...					
Task n	T_{na}	T_{nb}	$(T_{na} - T_{nb})$	F_n	$(T_{na} - T_{nb}) * F_n$

2.3.5 Drawbacks of Intel's Methodology

Following are some of the drawbacks discussed by others or found by myself in regards to Intel's EPMM:

As in Figure 6: Intel's Framework for Evaluating Employee Productivity page 64, not all employee activity data can be easily linked to financial aspects of an organization. Also, highly structured work settings are easier to quantify and compare than others, such knowledge workers (Gillar, 2004).

Further, in 5.7.4 Experiment Bias on page 136, I detail how bias may result from implementing the Intel methodology.

These are some of the shortcomings in Intel's methodology. But by considering the context, defining which variables to measure, and insisting on baseline as well as post-implementation measures, Intel has undoubtedly established a credible process for gathering productivity data. Therefore, this methodology will be utilized for my project's experiment.

Figure 6: Intel's Framework for Evaluating Employee Productivity

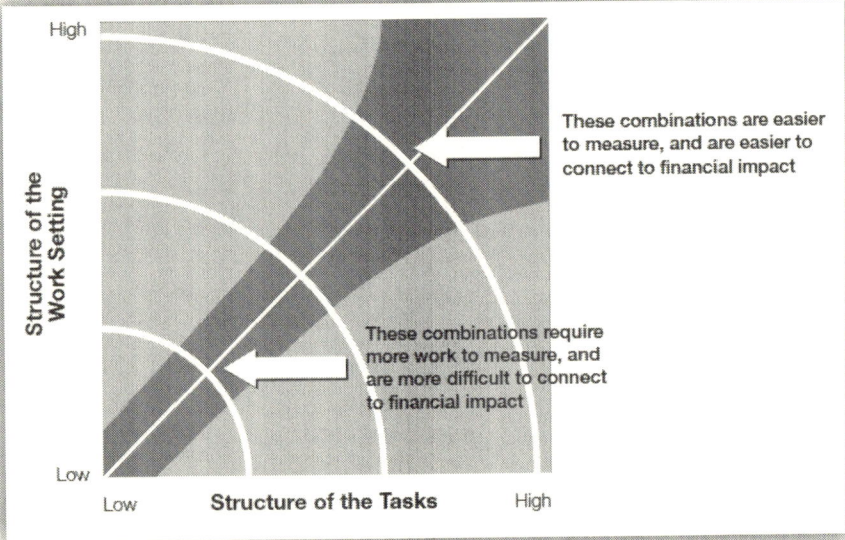

2.3.6   Benefits of Increased Employee Productivity

Research firms such as Intel claim that no magic formula exists for measuring the business value of productivity gains. Though Intel has established a framework for placing a value on employee time-savings, in their own research findings, Intel state that employee productivity benefits don't always translate into financial benefits, simply because financial valuations are made at an organizational level while productivity improvements are usually made at the process level. Many variables come into play between the process and organizational levels. In some cases, these other variables can mask the benefits of productivity gains.

If the IT solution was aimed at non-strategic processes, employee productivity gains might exist but not generate a significant financial benefit. In other cases, the IT implementation may only partially support the work processes.

With Open Source software, the financial benefits gained through the "no upfront cost" or "negligible costs" models provided by Open Source solutions are a concrete and measurable reality. The issue presented at hand would be whether any productivity *loss* exists with the implementation of such solutions that would negate those financial benefits, as implicitly stated by Scott (see Research Problem on page 20 here).

If we can link employee productivity *time-savings* gained through implementing Open Source solutions to one of the intermediate variables, such as cycle-time reduction, headcount reduction, or greater output, we can also consider these productivity gains to have – in themselves - a significant, positive financial impact as well.

2.3.7 Productivity vs. Usability

Productivity is one component of usability, but an important one that has to be measured with an experienced user. One of the findings of usability studies at Oracle; productivity is best measured *after* the first exposure to an application. The initial use would be characterized as measuring ease-of-learning, as the user is getting acquainted with the interface. Whereas each subsequent use becomes a better measure of productivity itself (Sauro, et al., 2008).

3. RESEARCH METHODOLOGY

3.1 Research Design

The main goals of the study design were to achieve the following objectives:

1. Research the most common organizational desktop software required and the available OSS alternatives to satisfy such requirements.
2. Verify previous findings locally through a survey questionnaire.
3. Build organizational desktop software solutions – both proprietary and Open Source - incorporating the findings of phases 1 and 2 above.
4. Execute an experiment utilizing a standard testing script for each subject to implement on both solutions of phase 3, with the means to measure user productivity during implementation of script instructions. Through subject observation, more reliable results are output.
5. Gather post-experiment data through interviews and a second survey questionnaire with the experiment subjects.

Accordingly, the following aspects were incorporated into this research as part of each milestone's design.

3.2 Phase 1: Research OSS Organizational Desktop Applications

In the organizational world, the Open Source Software's solutions portfolio has yet to produce products that compete with niche masters in a few areas such as Autodesk's AutoCAD (Wolfe, 2007). These "missing links" fortunately do not usually represent mainstream needs in most industries, but rather they are specific to a certain area of an industry as can be seen with evidence in this and other chapters of this study, especially within the cases related in 2.2 "Organizational Adoption of Open Source Desktop Software" on page 42. It is because of this reason that it is necessary to direct the study's scope towards where desktop software can best fit mainstream organizational needs.

This phase prepares for the core experiment within this study (Phase 3), where I need to present a solution containing a viable selection of alternative OSS applications for any organizational need. In order for this selection to be scientifically based and appropriately accepted by the widest possible user base, two preliminary questions have to be answered within this phase:

a) What are the common organizational needs for desktop application software ?

b) What are the best alternative OSS applications to suffice the previous needs ?

3.2.1   Research Instrument

For the purpose of this research, periodicals and journals were searched for successful implementation cases of migrations to Open Source Software solutions in organizations falling within the scope of this study (see Organizational Adoption of Open Source Desktop Software page 42). This is also in order to form a basis of what those organizations had actually targeted and benefited from in terms of the desktop Open Source *software types* and *actual products*.

Meticulous detail was followed in order to separate hype from fact in this area through targeting follow-up research articles and relying on multiple sources from both critics as well as advocates of OSS.

The end result has helped to understand the needs and requirements of diverse organizations, as well as the methodologies, applications, and tools they had used in order to successfully migrate to an Open Source Software solution. It most especially emphasized the applications that were accepted by end users in these cases.

Much of the results from the different environments depicted in the case studies had revolved around specific software products, which has given the results further credibility as they seem to support each other.

To further aid the cause of building credible results, the literature review has been followed by a research of polls related to preferred Open Source Software within many areas and across a wide user base. These results also lent support to the previous research and brought to focus how the Open Source experiment platform would need to be built.

3.3 Phase 2: Local Verification Survey

As the study is geared towards localizing results for the Arabian Gulf region and the Kingdom of Bahrain in particular, a locally-administered survey was prepared and utilized as part of its verification process. The survey was carefully administered in order to verify the most-used organizational desktop software types in relation to the Arab-speaking region in particular, and specifically the Arabian Gulf country of Bahrain.

3.3.1 Research Instrument

The survey questionnaire used as the instrument for this phase – a sample of which can be seen in Appendix C on page 169 - intends to profile respondents and gather feedback on what computer applications and functions employees use most frequently on their computers for work-related tasks in regional organizations.

This localized information will be used with the previous research done on most prevalent desktop applications on a global scale in order to build the third – or experiment - phase of the project.

The survey profiles users with a set of queries posed as both check-box answered as well as open-ended questions.

The actual survey then starts with a simple instruction rather than any introduction to its objectives since it aims to direct and not to guide the respondent. This is meant to preserve response objectivity.

The survey first directs respondents to the areas most frequently neglected by non-technical users through easy checkbox-answered questions. It then poses the core open-ended question for them to answer at the very end.

The anonymity of the survey serves to encourage frank answers, as respondents may fear they are leaking business secrets, and the short length and "pen and paper" approaches aim to encourage rapid and full completion of the questions.

Since it focuses on gathering localized data, the survey is available in both the local Arabic language as well as English. This is in order to overcome any language barriers within the respondent population.

The survey questionnaire was tested first on a small sample of 4 respondents and the format and instructions were accordingly changed slightly to compensate for errors found with some due to miscommunication of instructions.

3.3.2   Survey Population

From the Gartner Research statistics provided on page 17, we can calculate the professional and work-related desktop computer users worldwide at approximately 619,807,500.

For the survey part of this study, convenience of sampling was available through the student population where I teach. Through my work at the Arab Open University, I interact with students who are mostly full-time employees who have come back to part-time education in order to finish their college degree during their career involvement.

This environment has provided a wide sample range within many criteria, including: age, gender, technical proficiency, industry area, and job expertise.

3.3.3 Sampling Procedure

My procedure considered that as an IT lecturer, the IT major students whom I mostly teach usually posses higher technical proficiency. In order to prevent the perceived bias of utilizing such a sample, and hence negatively affecting the validity of results, the questionnaire was instead distributed through the General Studies tutors whose students are a mix relating to all majors in the University.

As described in detail on page 27, the study scope is restricted to organization-related and not personal or entertainment needs of individuals. The study also excludes the activities of non-employees who use the technology infrastructure of an organization, such as students in educational establishments, as their productivity does not directly affect the organization's profitability.

Yet, as desktop computers play different roles in many individuals' lives today, usually depending on where they are being used, the sampling procedure could include a wider range of users than usually permitted in such an educational environment. In fact, in this study, the actual sample includes any desktop computer user of minimum employment qualification who is able to use the application types installed on the desktop solutions created for this study's experiment.

In order to calculate the confidence interval gained from the 142 respondent sample size, I used the Sample Size Calculator from Creative Research Systems. The calculator depends on the following formula:

Sample Size

$$SS = \frac{Z^2 * (p) * (1-p)}{c^2}$$

Where:

Z = Z value (e.g. 1.96 for 95% confidence level)
p = percentage picking a choice, expressed as decimal
(.5 used for sample size needed)
c = confidence interval, expressed as decimal
(e.g., .04 = ±4)

Correction for Finite Population

$$new\ SS = \frac{SS}{1 + \frac{SS-1}{pop}}$$

Where: pop = population

For the previously estimated population of 619,807,500 users at a confidence level of 95% and a predicted response percentage of 50%, our 142 respondents would give us a confidence interval of 8.22 as shown by the calculator below.

Figure 7: Calculating the Survey's Confidence Interval

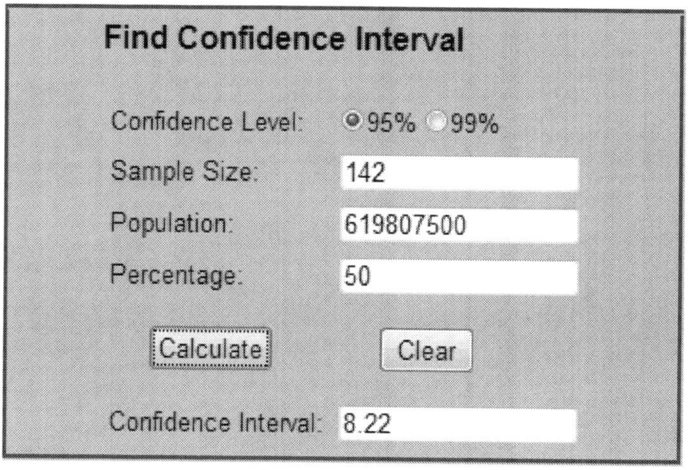

Find Confidence Interval

Confidence Level:	◉ 95% ○ 99%
Sample Size:	142
Population:	619807500
Percentage:	50

[Calculate] [Clear]

Confidence Interval: 8.22

(Creative Research Systems, 2009)

3.4   Phase 3: Build Desktop Software Solutions

In order to perform the required experiment in Phase 4 of this study, I need to prepare comparative desktop software solutions, one based on OSS and the other based on the current de facto standard of Microsoft products.

The solutions will also need to be benchmarked, and this will require a benchmarking tool to fulfill this purpose.

Both solutions are geared towards organizational requirements and as such need to make use of the demonstrated results of phases 1 and 2.

3.4.1   Research Instrument

In order to level the comparison hardware at a very low cost, an Open Source software-based machine virtualizer called VirtualBox was used. This virtual machine software was created by Sun Microsystems. Version 2.2.2 of VirtualBox was used for the experiment, the latest at the time.

When run in "full-screen mode", subjects cannot discern any visible difference between a natively running Operating System from one running within a virtual machine.

Also, to reliably output valid comparison results, a standard hardware specification was created for all virtual machines. Two virtual machines were created, as I required one for the OSS solution and another for the proprietary solution. Both were configured with the exact virtualized specifications and settings as detailed in Figure 8.

Figure 8: Virtual Machine Hardware Specifications Used

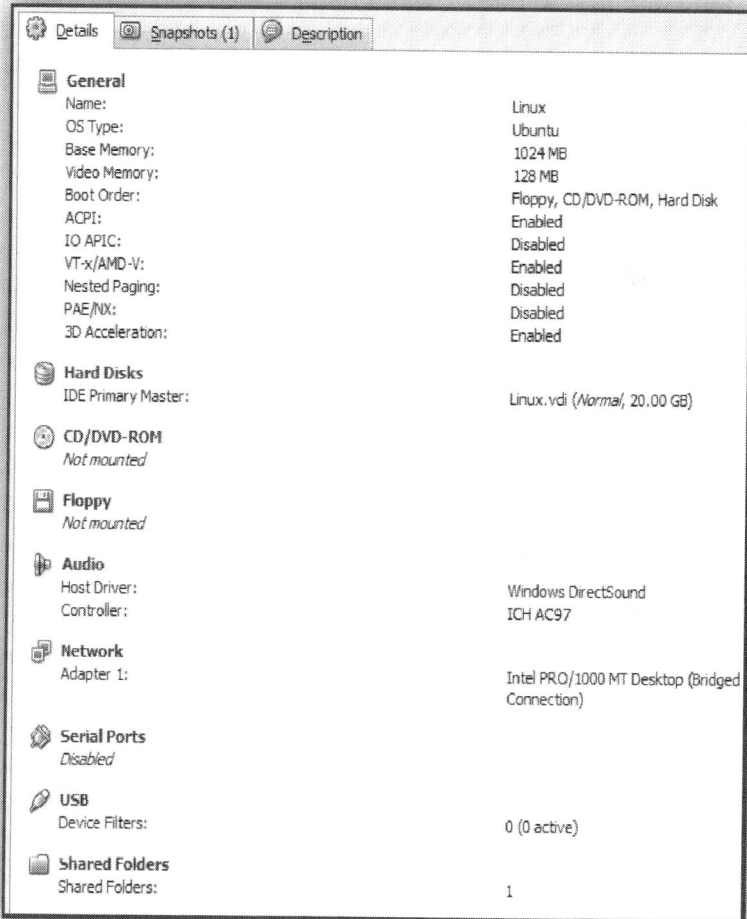

3.4.2 Installation and Configuration of OSS Solution

As per the results of phase 1 and 2 findings (discussed later in chapters 4 and 5 of this study), the Ubuntu Linux distribution has proven user-friendly, most popular, and highly supportable in an organizational environment. As such, it was chosen as the Operating System to base the OSS comparison solution upon.

Ubuntu version 9.04 was installed on the first VirtualBox virtual machine using Ubuntu's guided setup default options. Other applications found to be required through the results of the previous phases; 1 and 2 are: the PDF viewer (Document Viewer 2.26.1), the web browser (Firefox version 3.0.9), the word processor, presentation, and spreadsheet applications (OpenOffice.org version 3.0.1), the e-mail and calendaring/scheduling application (Evolution version 2.26.1). All part of the Ubuntu distribution and required no further installation steps.

As organizational desktop computers are usually delivered pre-configured to employees, configuration took place on the Ubuntu desktop solution in order to deliver an easier experience to first-time Windows users as they are migrated to Ubuntu Linux. Changes from the default settings took place in the following aspects, and as many may not be familiar with how these changes are done in Ubuntu Linux, screen captures are included in place of lengthy procedure explanations in Appendix D: Detailed Installation and Configuration of OSS Solution on page 171. A summary of the previous follows:

- Installed the VirtualBox Linux Additions in order to enable features such as "Shared Folders".
- Created a start.sh file which includes the following command line to map the shared folder: sudo

mount.vboxsf New /home/test/Desktop/Start. This is in order to map the shared folder "New" to the mount point "/home/test/Desktop/Start". The Intaj productivity benchmark will be run from this shared folder.

- The dual taskbar layout was changed to a single taskbar layout as Windows users were more accustomed to the later.
- Taskbar main menu was edited in order to simplify the number of available applications to the user.
- Changed the File Management default view to "List View".
- Configured the keyboard's Windows Key to start the taskbar's main menu.
- Mouse pointer size was increased.
- Installed Arabic language related additions except for translations.
- Added the Arabic (Bahrain) keyboard layout.
- Configured the keyboard layout switching controls.
- Added the "Keyboard Indicator" panel to the taskbar.
- Installed extra free fonts through the "Ubuntu restricted extras" package.
- All the latest Ubuntu software updates and patches were applied automatically.
- Installed Sun Java Runtime Environment 6.0 and Browser Plug-in.
- Installed Adobe Flash 10 Browser Plug-in.

- Configured OpenOffice.org options to enable support for Complex Text Layout (CTL). Necessary for Arabic text input.

- Configured all CTL basic fonts in OpenOffice.org to AlMohanad 14pt except "Heading" which was configured at 16pt.

- The Evolution e-mail client was setup.

- Installed the Mint Menu through Synaptics after adding "deb http://packages.linuxmint.com gloria main" to the sources. This menu replaced the default Gnome menu on the panel (taskbar).

- Installed wallpaperr and the Mac OS X theme from http://gnome-look.org

3.4.3 Installation and Configuration of the Microsoft Solution

As the study involves comparing two migration scenarios from the currently retired Microsoft Operating System (Windows Xp); one to the OSS alternative and the other to the Microsoft prescribed solution, the latest version of Windows Vista (Service Pack 1) was installed on the second virtual machine using the default setup configuration options.

For comparison purposes, the latest Microsoft Office 2007 suite of applications was also installed, containing the word processor, spreadsheet, presentation, and e-mail/calendaring applications. Microsoft Windows Vista already contains the necessary web browser application (Internet Explorer 7). All applications were installed with the default configuration.

After installing all of the above, the following configuration changes took place:

- Installed the VirtualBox Windows Additions in order to enable features such as "Shared Folders".
- Created a shared folder named father and mapped the Z: drive in Windows Vista to \\vboxsvr\New. The Intaj productivity benchmark will be run from this shared folder.
- Disabled the Windows Sidebar.
- Mouse pointer size was increased.
- Disabled "Hide file extensions for known file types" in Folder Options.
- Added the Arabic(Bahrain) keyboard layout; Arabic (101).
- Changed the default code-page for non-Unicode applications to Arabic(Bahrain) in "Regional Settings".
- Installed Sun Java Runtime Environment 6.0 and Browser Plug-in.
- Installed Adobe Flash 10 Browser Plug-in.
- Installed Adobe Reader 9.1.
- Installed the Office 2007 "Save as PDF/XPS" Add-in.
- The Outlook e-mail client was setup with the following e-mail server settings in order to be able to send and receive e-mail:

    Username: the_test@live.com

    Password: desktop

    Incoming server: pop3.live.com

Use secure connection: SSL

Authentication type: password

Outgoing server: smtp.live.com

Use Secure Connection: TLS Encryption

Authentication Type: Login

- Installed the Office 2007 Arabic Multi-User Interface (MUI) for additional Arabic fonts and spell-check capabilities.

Benchmarking Windows Vista can be difficult because the operating system is attempting to improve itself over time based on observed usage patterns. Windows Vista presents even greater challenges than earlier versions of Windows because the system's behavior changes when user input is detected, when battery power states change, and based on other default and user-defined policies (Microsoft Corp. , 2007).

Microsoft has published a guide to help measure real-world performance of the Windows Vista operating system. The guide states:

Typically, you should choose to benchmark systems with the default settings created during Windows Vista installation, which matches most users' experience.

Two critical performance issues pointed out in the guide, which require special consideration and preparation before measurement, are:

1. Training the system: As data for routine tasks is pre-fetched for better performance, the system has to be trained by:
   a. installing all programs necessary for benchmarking
   b. rebooting twice with a 5-minute login between reboots
   c. running the benchmark workload multiple times beforehand
2. Enforcing idle-time tasks to run: For indexing of file locations and file placement optimization, the system will usually wait for an idle period for a maximum of 3 days before running these tasks. Therefore, and in order not to negatively impact running benchmarks, it is necessary to execute the following statement in a command line to enforce idle-time tasks to run before measuring performance:

Rundll32.exe
advapi32.dll,ProcessIdleTasks

(Microsoft Corp. , 2007).

3.5   Phase 4: Executing the Experiment

The core of this study is to discover the impact of migrating to an OSS desktop software solution on employee productivity in any organization.

The preliminary research and survey questionnaire were meant to find out what types of applications I needed subjects to use for my experiment and what specific applications were best suited to fulfill those subject needs.

The two desktop software solutions previously built were meant for comparison of results in two different scenarios. One scenario being the adherence to the status quo of Microsoft proprietary products, while the other diverges to a complete OSS alternative.

Now comes the moment where I tap the actual problem at hand through an experiment designed to gather data representing the productivity of subjects in each of the two solution scenarios previously built.

How we measure employee productivity and compare a set of productivity data to another is the subject matter of this critical design stage.

3.5.1   Research Instrument

The main quantitative methodology in this data gathering phase is based on Intel's EPMM (Employee Productivity Measurement Methodology) which I had already discussed previously to some degree of length on page 55. But as the EPMM encompasses a relatively wider number of scenarios, I will simply point out here the areas of Intel's methodology required for this study.

The study maps to the four phases of Intel's methodology as follows:

- Phase 1 - Exploration: discussed in Phase 1: Research OSS Organizational Desktop Applications on page 68 and Phase 2: Local Verification Survey page 71 of this study.

- Phase 2 - Preparation: discussed in Phase 3: Build Desktop Software Solutions page 76 of this study.

- Phase 3 – Data Collection: discussed in Phase 4: Executing the Experiment on page 84 of this study and Phase 5: Post-Experiment Data Gathering on page 97 of this study.

- Phase 4 – Data Analysis and Reporting: will be discussed in chapter 4 on page 100 and chapter 5 on page 126 of this study.

The EPMM components used in this phase of the study include an experiment and an observation of experiment subjects.

3.5.2 Experiment

The experiment is built according to the Intel EPMM concept of measuring employee productivity, where tacko arc timed and the less the time taken the more productive an employee is considered.

In this context, in order to compare the productivity of employees using two different software solutions, we would therefore aim to measure the time taken to complete an identical set of common tasks performed by the same employee on the same hardware platform for each of the software solutions. The average of measured time for a larger number of experiment subjects would render more valid results. Also, the higher the number of experiment subjects, the more valid the study findings will be.

The experiment starts by briefing the subjects with the objectives of the experiment and what will be presented to them throughout in summary.

The subjects are then given the experiment machine with the Microsoft Windows Vista virtual machine started and the Intaj productivity benchmark running.

The decision to start with the Windows platform was in order to level the handicaps between the two scenarios. If we start with Windows, the subjects will be in an environment they are more accustomed with, handling the challenge of familiarizing themselves with the test script. When the subjects are given the Linux environment, they will have accustomed themselves to the test script but faced with the new challenge of familiarizing themselves with Linux. If we had started with Linux, the subjects would have had the double challenge of familiarizing themselves with both the new test script as well as the new computing environment.

The subjects are introduced to the way Intaj works and are given 10 minutes to accustom themselves with the computing environment before starting the execution of the test script either in English or in Arabic as listed in Appendix G: Test Script Files: Arabic and English page 191.

Once the script tasks are completed for the Windows Vista solution, the subjects are introduced to the Ubuntu Linux virtual machine with Intaj running on it as well. Again, the subjects are allowed to spend 10 minutes of time getting accustomed to the computing environment before starting the execution of the test script activities.

The experiment script aims to test the following common tasks:

1. Navigating the file and folder system
2. Copying files
3. Opening word processing documents
4. Creating documents
5. Saving documents
6. Printing documents
7. Copying document content
8. Pasting document content
9. Writing using the Arabic language keyboard
10. Sending an e-mail
11. Attaching a document to an e-mail
12. Using formatting features of a word-processor

As each experiment subject completes their tasks, and before another subject starts working on the virtual machine, the virtual machine is first reverted to a previous "snapshot" state, saved before the work of the experiment subject had started. This is in order to ensure the validity of results through standardization of each subject's environment and preventing the experiment environment from being affected by preceding use. Snapshots are a feature of virtual machines such as VirtualBox.

The revert process does not affect the log files saved by Intaj. Intaj is run from the "Shared Folder" feature of the virtual machine, where the folder appears inside the virtual machine, but the contents actually reside on the native host which runs the guest virtual machine.

The two log files created by running Intaj on the two virtual machines are moved from the Intaj folder to a subfolder named after the experiment subject. Only then will the experiment be started with the next subject.

The experiment was tested first on a small sample of 8 subjects and the format and instructions were accordingly changed slightly to compensate for difficulties found with some subjects due to miscommunication of instructions.

3.5.3   Experiment Population

From the Gartner Research statistics provided on page 17, we can calculate the professional and work-related desktop computer users worldwide at approximately 619,807,500.

For the experiment part of this study, convenience of sampling was available through the student population where I teach. Through my work at the Arab Open University, I interact with students who are mostly employees who have come back to education in order to finish their college degree during their career involvement.

This environment has provided a wide sample range within many criteria, including: age, gender, technical proficiency, industry area, and job expertise.

3.5.4 Sampling Procedure

My procedure considered that as an IT lecturer, the IT major students whom I mostly teach usually posses higher technical proficiency. Therefore, in order to prevent the perceived bias of utilizing such a sample, and hence negatively affecting the validity of results, the sampling took place by selecting equal numbers of students from each study major in the University.

As described in detail on page 27, the study scope is restricted to organization-related and not personal or entertainment needs of individuals. The study also excludes the activities of non-employees who use the technology infrastructure of an organization, such as students in educational establishments, as their productivity does not directly affect the organization's profitability.

Yet, as desktop computers play different roles in many individuals' lives today, usually depending on where they are being used, the sampling procedure could include a wider range of subjects than usually permitted in such an educational environment. In fact, in this study, the actual sample includes any desktop computer user of minimum employment qualification who is able to use the application types installed on the desktop solutions created for this study's experiment.

In order to calculate the required sample size for the experiment, I used the Sample Size Calculator from Creative Research Systems. The calculator depends on the following formula:

Sample Size

$$SS = \frac{Z^2 * (p) * (1-p)}{c^2}$$

Where:

Z = Z value (e.g. 1.96 for 95% confidence level)
p = percentage picking a choice, expressed as decimal
(.5 used for sample size needed)
c = confidence interval, expressed as decimal
(e.g., .04 = ±4)

Correction for Finite Population

$$new\ SS = \frac{SS}{1 + \frac{SS-1}{pop}}$$

Where: pop = population

For the previously estimated population of 619,807,500 employee desktop users at a confidence level of 95% and a confidence interval of 5, we would require a sample size of 384 experiment subjects as shown by the calculator below.

Figure 9: Determining the Optimal Experiment Sample Size

Determine Sample Size

Confidence Level:	⦿ 95% ○ 99%
Confidence Interval:	5
Population:	619807500
[Calculate]	[Clear]
Sample size needed:	384

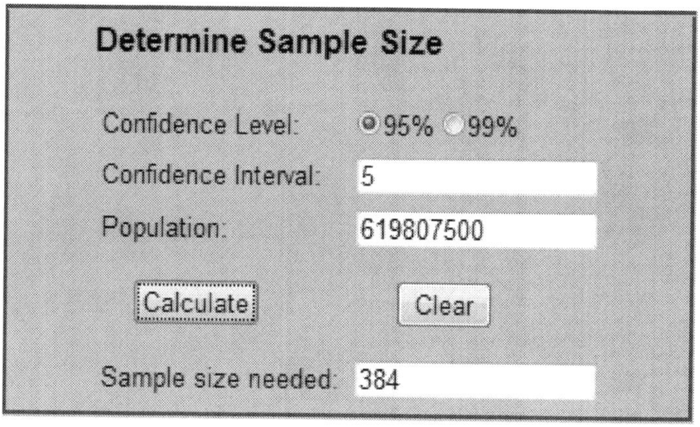

(Creative Research Systems, 2009)

My experiment sample size reached 52 within the available time and resources. Based on the previous calculator, this sample size is calculated to provide a confidence interval of 13.6 as shown in the figure below.

Find Confidence Interval

Confidence Level:	⦿ 95% ◯ 99%
Sample Size:	52
Population:	700000000
Percentage:	50
[Calculate]	[Clear]
Confidence Interval:	13.59

(Creative Research Systems, 2009)

3.5.5 The Benchmarking Utility (Intaj)

In order that a time measure can be taken for each required task in the experiment script, a small utility was developed which could assist the user with the script by showing each task that has to be executed by the user and allowing the user to record the time taken for each task of the script.

This utility was name "Intaj", the Arabic word for productivity, seeing as it has Arabic display capabilities in order to be more usable by native Arabic speakers. The utility is licensed under the "CC-GNU GPL version 2.0" Open Source license. The source code is listed in the Appendix: Source Code for "Intaj" (A Productivity Benchmark in Java page 183.

Intaj has a small movable window that at first shows a welcome message to the user which explains its purpose and how it can be used. All text shown in Intaj is extracted from a separate Unicode text file (artasks.txt), which is freely changeable by the administrator of the experiment, and - in Arabic mode – text is aligned right-to-left in the window.

Intaj has three buttons. Intaj's left-most button switches Intaj's language mode and also shows the current language mode; "Ar" for Arabic and "En" for English. In English mode, text instructions will be extracted from a different text file (entasks.txt) and will be aligned left-to-right. Both modes are bi-lingual and language characters can be mixed.

Intaj asks the user to start by pressing the right-most button, which will present the first task and instruct the user to press the right-most button again to start timing the task, and to press the middle button in order to stop timing the task. Once done with the first task, the user is immediately presented with the second task and same button sequence is performed once more. This cycle continues for all tasks in the text file representing the whole of the experiment's script activities.

The recorded times for each user are stored in a separate text log file named uniquely by using the start time in hours, minutes, and seconds. This log records the time for each task in the script as well as the total time taken to complete the script.

In order for Intaj to run uniformly on both Microsoft and Linux platforms, it has been written using the Java programming language for its portability. The Java runtime environment was previously installed on both virtual machines for this purpose.

Figure 11: Intaj Running in Arabic on Ubuntu Linux

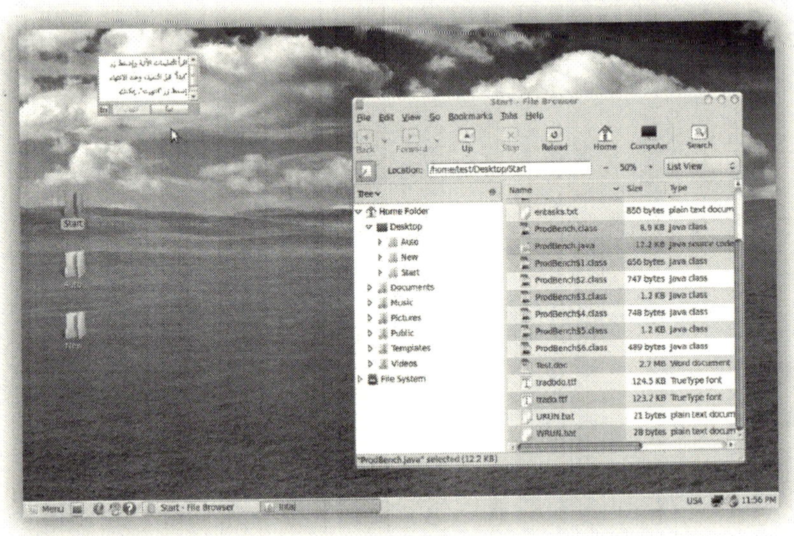

Figure 12: Intaj Running in English on Windows Vista

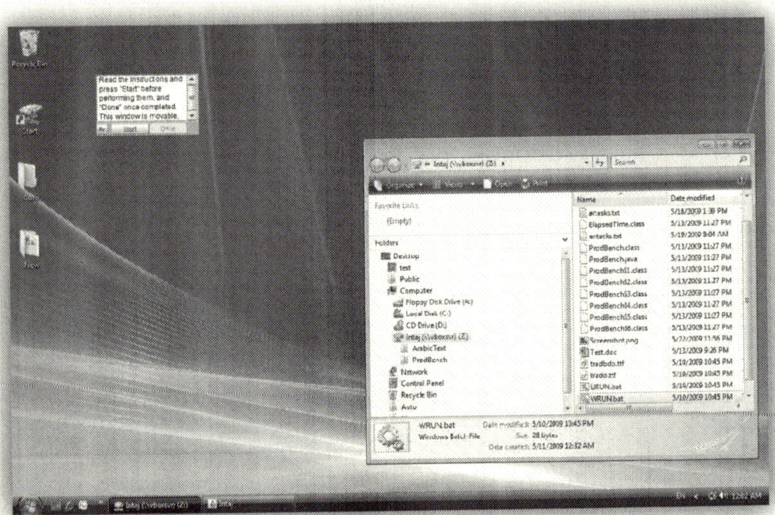

3.5.6 Observation

In order to gain further information from the experiment and -
more importantly – to preserve the validity and reliability of
results, subjects were observed as they worked through the
script. This is in order to benefit the experiment with the following
advantages:

- Ensure that subjects are actually performing the tasks,
  and that the tasks performed are to the required level of
  uniformity.
- Make sure subjects understand the instructions and that
  they are not a barrier to complete and that
  misunderstanding does not contributes to a task's
  execution time.
- Ensure consistent and proper use of Intaj throughout the
  experiment.

Subjects were reminded that observation does not mean
allowing dialogue or assistance requests. This was in order that
subjects focus solely on completing the tasks at hand and in a
fair manner between subjects.

Observation consumed time and effort as well as constraining
resources. It allowed much fewer subjects to be used for the
experiment from the calculated optimal number. The great
advantage gained was a deeper understanding of the case
scenarios each experiment went through and a much more valid
result than simple calculation can present. An example of this is

that of the 832 timings recorded within the experiment, only 4 timings of those tabulated were found to contain invalid values.

3.6 Phase 5: Post-Experiment Data Gathering

Feedback from experiment subjects is gathered in this phase in order to close with their final subjective thoughts and gain an insight into the user-perspective on both the experiment and the presented solutions.

3.6.1 Research Instrument

Two methodologies were used in this phase; an interview followed by a survey questionnaire, and both were short and concise.

3.6.2 Interview

After each subject finished their experiment, they were interviewed in order to gain an insight into their opinion of the solutions and how they thought each could be enhanced, most especially following points were posed to all subjects:

- What they liked of each solution presented to them
- What they disliked of each solution presented to them
- How willing they were to use one or the other solution in their actual work environment and why

The results of the interview questions were recorded on the same survey questionnaire form that is filled-in after the experiment, as detailed below.

3.6.3 Survey

Upon completing the experiment, subjects are surveyed for their opinions of the solutions presented. The survey form is an Excel worksheet which is filled-in by the experiment administrator and not the subject.

The survey starts by profiling respondents, and then gathers their feedback on the Linux and Microsoft solutions they were introduced to within the experiment.

The survey starts by profiling users through a set of queries posed as both check-box answered questions, as well as open-ended questions. The actual survey then starts with questions on both desktop software solutions. Following are the survey criteria and the values posed to respondents regarding each survey criteria:

- computer proficiency
  - 0 – No proficiency
  - 1 – Low proficiency
  - 2 – Medium proficiency
  - 3 – Expert proficiency
- ease of use of each solution:
  - 0 – Very Hard
  - 1 - Hard
  - 2 - Easy
  - 3 – Very easy
- satisfaction level with each solution
  - 0 - Not satisfied

- - 1 - Almost satisfied
  - 2 - Satisfied
  - 3 - Very satisfied
- preferred work solution
- like and dislikes of each solution

3.7 Data Collection and Analysis

Log files created by each virtual machine were saved in a separate folder for every experiment subject. As log files were of "comma-separated value" format (csv), they were accessed as separate spreadsheets and their values were tabulated into a single spreadsheet in the format shown in the appendix "Sample Tabulated Experiment Data" on page 182. The spreadsheet was checked for invalid timings and the 4 invalid entries found were deleted.

The preliminary survey's data was also tabulated from printed forms into a single spreadsheet.

All spreadsheets were imported by SPSS version 17 for analysis. In SPSS, all nominal variables were given values except for Name, Industry, Job, and Specialization. All variables were also given labels. The age variable was binned into four parts according to the Mean and +/-1 standard deviation. Frequency tables and charts were produced from the data.

A Paired Samples T-test analysis was implemented for the experiment data's task times. This is in order to verify if a statistical difference truly exists between the subject's productivity on the Vista system in comparison with the Linux system. This in turn answers the study's main problem.

The interview results were tabulated into quantifiable categories to form a frequency table based on keywords recorded from the interviewees. Similar phrases were summed under their related keyword based on the interviewer's understanding of the interviewee's main objective.

4. DATA ANALYSIS

4.1 Organizational Desktop Software Requirements

From the first survey in this study, preliminary data was gathered as to the major types of software required in organizations for their desktop computer applications.

Following are the graphs profiling the survey respondents based on the frequency tables from the survey results, as in Appendix I: Frequency Tables from Preliminary Survey on page 200.

Figure 13: Respondent Gender & Industry Profile from Preliminary Survey

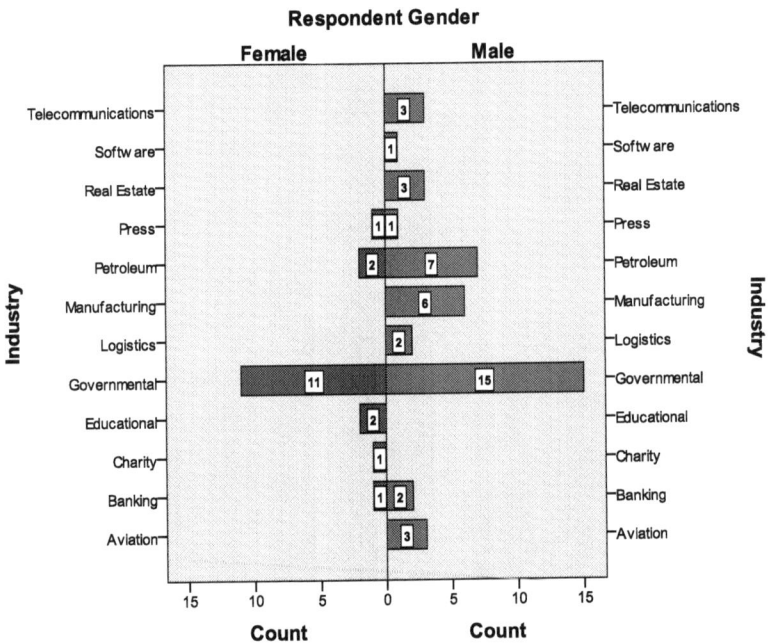

Figure 14: Respondent Proficiency & Age Group from Preliminary Survey

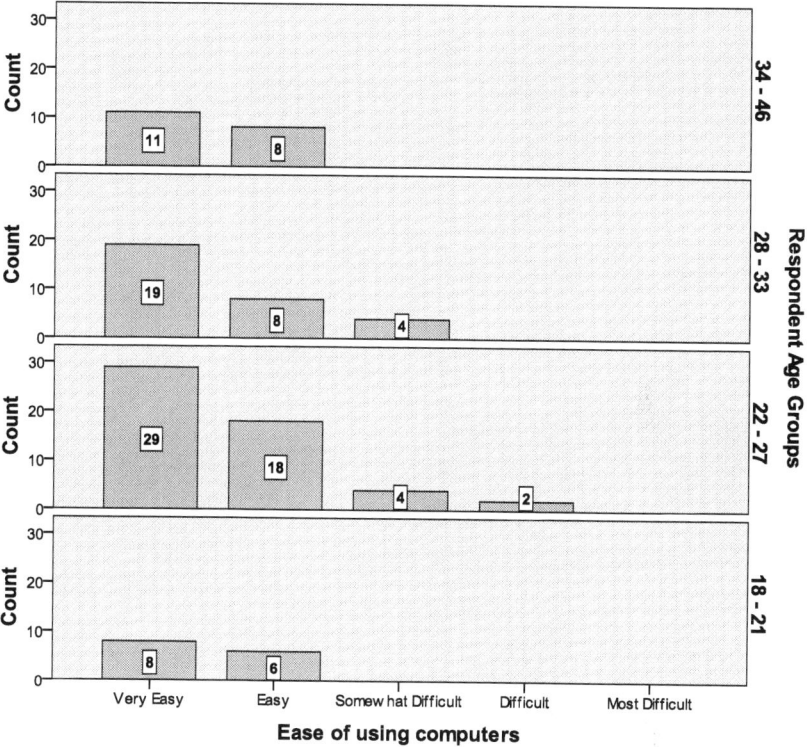

The survey's respondents were categorized as 59.2% male and 30.3% female, with 10.6% who did not declare their gender. Most respondents (57%) did not declare their work-related industry. Of the 69.8% who declared their work sector, most respondents (44.4%) worked in the private sector.

In respect to age, respondent ages were grouped based on the sample Mean and a standard deviation of +/-1. Twenty-five respondents (17.6%) had not declared their age. Of those who did, 37.3% fall into the 22-27 years category, 21.8% fall into the 28-33 years category, 13.4% fall into the 34-46 years category, and 9.9% fall into the 18-21 years category.

In regards to proficiency in computer use, the majority of respondents (88.7%) considered their experiences between "Easy" and "Very Easy". While 11.2% only considered their computer experiences to be either "Difficult" or "Somewhat Difficult".

The main purpose of this survey was to find the group of applications and functions required by most organizational employees.

In the range of 70% to 100% of respondents, the most needed application functions were found to be:

1. Printing documents (95.8%)
2. Communicating using e-mail (92.3%)
3. Web browsing (87.3%)
4. Reading PDF documents (83.8%)
5. Reading Arabic documents (79.6%)

In the range of 30% to 69% of respondents, the most needed application functions were found to be:

6. Accessing documents on a server through the organization's network (55.6%)
7. Uses a word-processing application (43.7%)
8. Producing spreadsheets (33.8%)

In the range of 10% to 29% of respondents, the most needed application functions were found to be:

9. Using the Microsoft Office suite of applications (22.5%)
10. Calendaring and scheduling (19%)
11. Using software to create presentations (18.3%)

All other requirements were in the range below 10% as in Figure 15: Ratio of Employee Desktop Software Requirements and as such disregarded for this study as they pertain to special and not general organizational use.

By categorizing the previous functions into their software components, we arrive at the conclusion that the main required functions fall within the following OSS software component types:

1. Linux operating system (for requirement numbers 1,4, and 6)
2. Office-like application suite (for requirement numbers 2,5,7,8,9,10 & 11)
3. Web browser (for requirement number 3)

The exact software components selected for my study's experiment is based on research of OSS Desktop Software Market Leaders on page 107.

Figure 15: Ratio of Employee Desktop Software Requirements

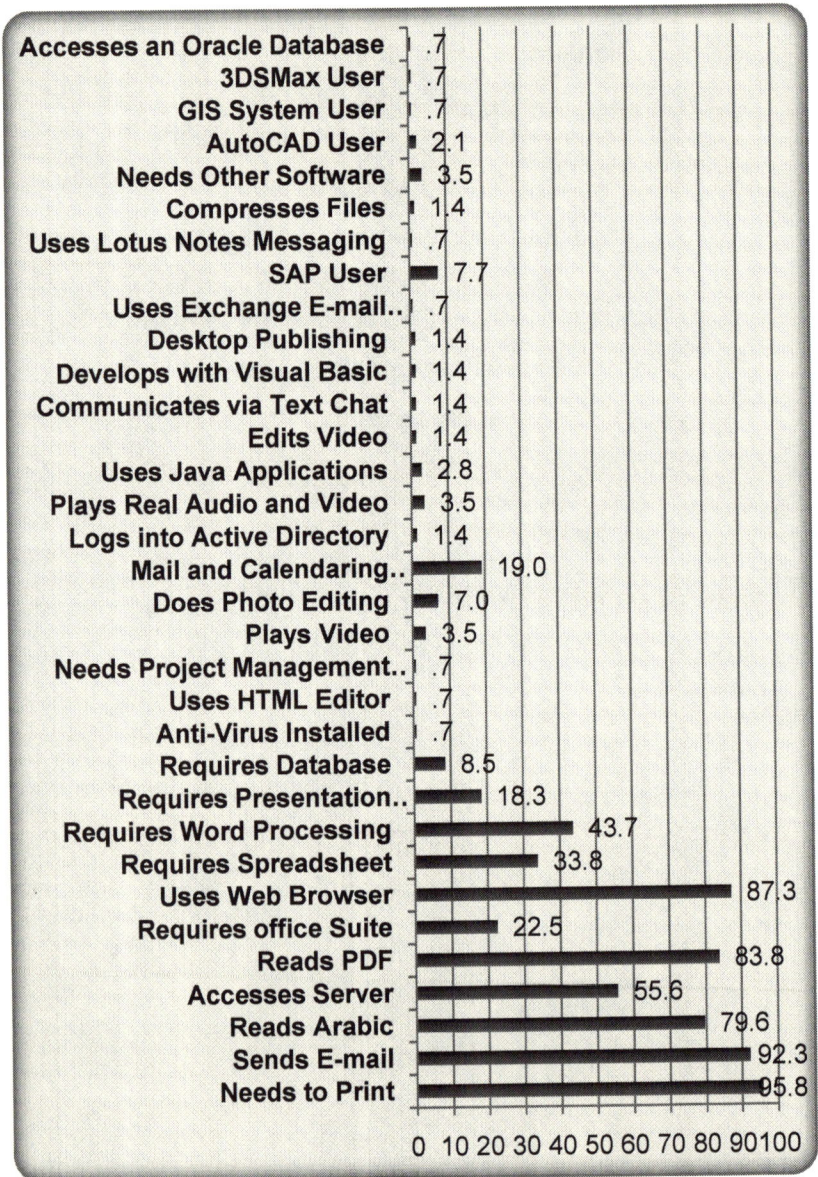

Accesses an Oracle Database	.7
3DSMax User	.7
GIS System User	.7
AutoCAD User	2.1
Needs Other Software	3.5
Compresses Files	1.4
Uses Lotus Notes Messaging	.7
SAP User	7.7
Uses Exchange E-mail..	.7
Desktop Publishing	1.4
Develops with Visual Basic	1.4
Communicates via Text Chat	1.4
Edits Video	1.4
Uses Java Applications	2.8
Plays Real Audio and Video	3.5
Logs into Active Directory	1.4
Mail and Calendaring..	19.0
Does Photo Editing	7.0
Plays Video	3.5
Needs Project Management..	.7
Uses HTML Editor	.7
Anti-Virus Installed	.7
Requires Database	8.5
Requires Presentation..	18.3
Requires Word Processing	43.7
Requires Spreadsheet	33.8
Uses Web Browser	87.3
Requires office Suite	22.5
Reads PDF	83.8
Accesses Server	55.6
Reads Arabic	79.6
Sends E-mail	92.3
Needs to Print	95.8

4.2   OSS Desktop Software Market Leaders

The OSS market utilizes a different product metaphor. As the main initiative for software production is not material, the operating system and applications are rolled into one installable software solution package called a "distribution". Depending on the authoring party, each distribution will choose its own collection of software packages, and usually multiple options are included to suffice different users' needs and tastes. Further research into available Open Source software solutions shows no lack in distribution options, and some have been rapidly taking high market shares in recent years.

Figure 16: Linux market trend, from Market Share by Net Applications

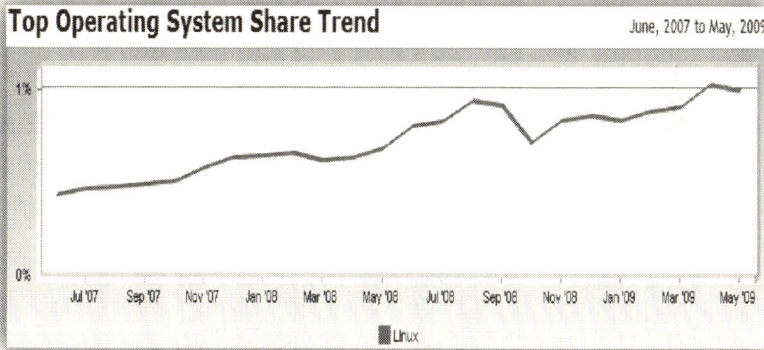

For the sake of simplicity to the reader, I still studied each of the following components in the usual modular fashion in order to choose the market leaders for the experiment part of this study.

4.2.1   Operating Systems

The 3 most popular Linux distributions since 2006 all offer corporate paid support options; Ubuntu, Novell's openSUSE, and Redhat's Fedora. Of these, Ubuntu specifically has gained a wider audience than any other competitive distribution (Bodnar, 2009). This popularity is an important product factor for organizations in terms of range of support community, quantity of feedback to developers, and product development sustainability.

Of 141,033 registrations of installed distributions recorded by the Linux Counter Machine project, the following ratios for Linux Distributions shows Ubuntu's Linux market leadership at 20.22% (Linux Counter, 2009).

Table 1: Linux Counter's Linux Distribution Usage Ratios

Distribution	Count	Percent	
arch linux	716	0.51%	
centos	1642	1.16%	
debian	25136	17.82%	
debian lenny	1417	1.00%	
fedora core	9365	6.64%	
gentoo	10327	7.32%	
kubuntu	2339	1.66%	
mandrake	4890	3.47%	
mandriva	2934	2.08%	
red hat	7963	5.65%	
s.u.s.e	12266	8.70%	
slackware	10668	7.56%	
ubuntu	28512	20.22%	
Others	26101	18.51%	

Also, 38,500 voters submitted their views in 2007 to the Desktop Linux Market survey and Ubuntu ranked first with a ratio of

30.3% (Desktop Linux, 2007). While the near-5000 voters for the Linux Journal's 2009 Reader's Choice Awards garnered Ubuntu the "Favorite Primary Linux Distribution of Choice" by 45% of votes, gaining ahead of its previous year's win of 37% (Gray, 2009).

4.2.2 Application Suites

Multiple substitutes exist for the Microsoft Office suite of applications in the OSS arena. The Linux Journal's 2009 Reader's Choice Awards shows the OpenOffice.org suite to be the most popular with an overwhelming 85% vote, the exact same ratio garnered by the suite in the 2008 Reader's Choice Awards. The closest competitor - KOffice – got no more than 3% of votes (Gray, 2009).

The Openoffice.org project statistics page shows 98,308,686 downloads to date in order to hint at the extent of success the multi-platform multi-language application has enjoyed to date (OpenOffice.org, 2009).

4.2.3 Web Browsers

Seven popular OSS web browser applications are currently in active development (Blanco, 2009). But it is the Mozilla Firefox web browser that currently owns the popular vote for this OSS application segment according to actual usage information by W3Counter (W3Counter, 2009), and Market Share (Net Applications, 2009) which place its usage at 30.7% and 21.53% respectively, and current results of the on-going long-term survey conducted by SurveyWare (SurveyWare, 2009) which placed satisfaction for Firefox at 67.31%. Their details can be seen in Appendix H: "Research Data Figures" on page 192.

Microsoft's Internet Explorer – which does not run natively in Linux - is in a unique position as it is distributed automatically with the Windows operating system, ensuring a large chunk of the web browser market share for Microsoft automatically.

Yet, the highest user satisfaction rate since 2004 has been for the Mozilla Firefox web browser according to SurveyWare, where the Firefox browser garnered 63.27% of the votes in comparison with other familiar web browsers such Internet Explorer, Opera, Safari, and Chrome (SurveyWare, 2009).

The high satisfaction and relatively high adoption rate have been attributed to the unique extensibility feature to Firefox's functions through its "add-on" architecture, which enables faster addition of features to the browser (gHacks.net, 2009).

An example would be the "Speed Dial" feature introduced in the Opera web browser since version 9.2 as a major change (Cabello, 2007). This version was released on April 11th 2007 (VersionTracker, 2008), the extension with similar functionality for Firefox was released 4 days later (Rio, 2009).

The Firefox web browser has been coveted "Favorite Web Browser" in the previously mentioned Linux Journal 2009 Reader's Choice Awards, with an 87% share of votes. No other desktop application earned as many votes in any of the award's categories (Gray, 2009). Desktop Linux's 2007 polls also ranked Firefox as the browser of choice for 59.6% of voters (Desktop Linux, 2007).

Figure 17: Web browser and operating system stats from W3Counter (January 2009)

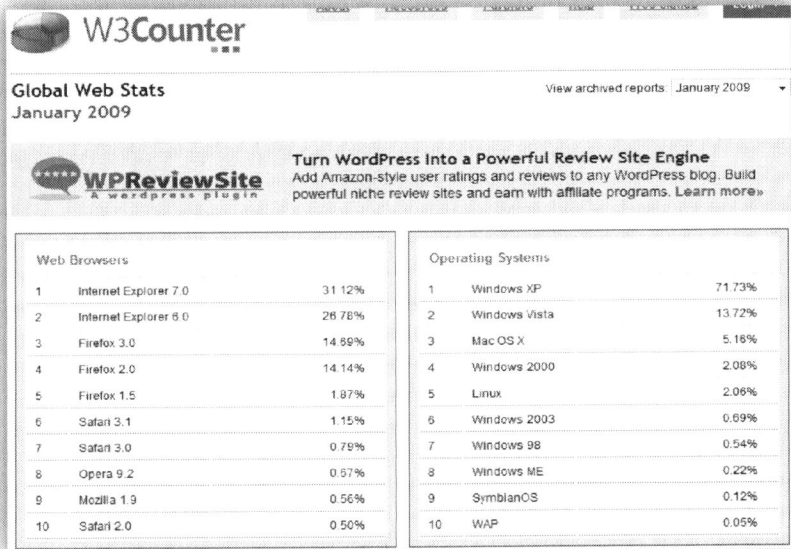

W3Counter

Global Web Stats
January 2009

View archived reports: January 2009

WPReviewSite *A wordpress plugin*

Turn WordPress Into a Powerful Review Site Engine
Add Amazon-style user ratings and reviews to any WordPress blog. Build powerful niche review sites and earn with affiliate programs. Learn more»

Web Browsers		
1	Internet Explorer 7.0	31.12%
2	Internet Explorer 6.0	26.78%
3	Firefox 3.0	14.69%
4	Firefox 2.0	14.14%
5	Firefox 1.5	1.87%
6	Safari 3.1	1.15%
7	Safari 3.0	0.79%
8	Opera 9.2	0.67%
9	Mozilla 1.9	0.56%
10	Safari 2.0	0.50%

Operating Systems		
1	Windows XP	71.73%
2	Windows Vista	13.72%
3	Mac OS X	5.16%
4	Windows 2000	2.08%
5	Linux	2.06%
6	Windows 2003	0.69%
7	Windows 98	0.54%
8	Windows ME	0.22%
9	SymbianOS	0.12%
10	WAP	0.05%

Figure 18: Browser market share (from Market Share by Net Applications)

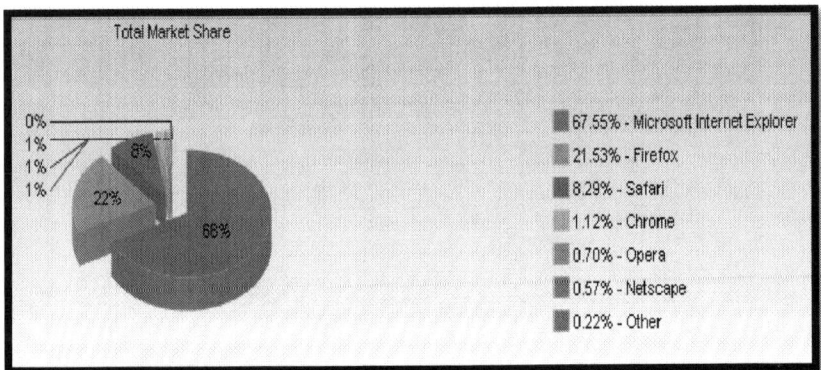

Total Market Share

- 67.55% - Microsoft Internet Explorer
- 21.53% - Firefox
- 8.29% - Safari
- 1.12% - Chrome
- 0.70% - Opera
- 0.57% - Netscape
- 0.22% - Other

112

Figure 19: Browser satisfaction poll results

Aug. 2008 – Feb. 2009 (by SurveyWare)

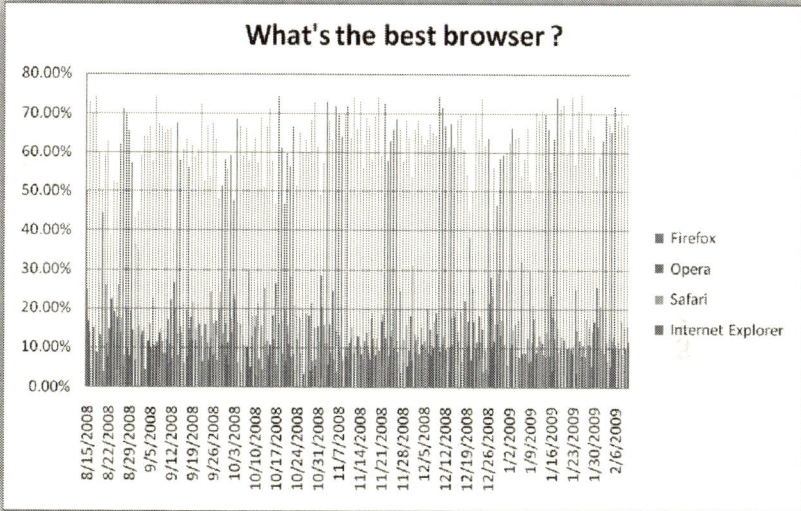

Figure 20: Geographical dispersion of satisfaction poll respondents (by SurveyWare)

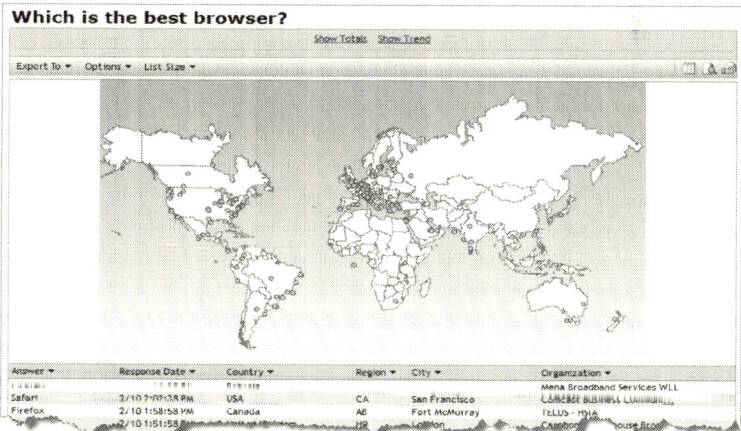

4.2.4   Other Supporting Research

The selection of Open Source desktop software selected to fulfill the organizational needs uncovered by the study's first survey and utilized in this study's experiment depended on the previously mentioned research results. The selection is further supported by the Business Readiness Rating organization's GRAM (Generally Recognized As Mature) list as all of the selected Open Source software (Ubuntu operating system and the OpenOffice.org and Firefox applications) are included within that list (Business Readiness Rating, 2006).

Further, the successful migration scenarios mentioned in "Organizational Adoption of Open Source Desktop Software" on page 42 had done their own research and arrived at results detailed in the following table. These also helped shape the decision for choosing the experiment's Open Source operating system and applications as well.

Table 2: Summary of Desktop OSS Adoption Case Studies

Country	Body	Operating System	App. Suite	Browser
Belgium	Belgian Ministry of Justice	Suse	OpenOffice.org	
Cuba	Cuban Government	Nova (Gentoo based)	OpenOffice.org	Firefox
Ecuador	Public Administration	Elastix		
France	Gendarmerie Nationale	Ubuntu	OpenOffice.org	Firefox
	PSA Peugeot Citroën	Suse	OpenOffice.org	Firefox
Germany	City of Munich	LiMux (Debian based)	OpenOffice.org	Firefox
	Foreign Ministry	Debian	OpenOffice.org	
India	Tamil Nadu government	Suse	OpenOffice.org	Firefox
Malaysia	Government of Malaysia		OpenOffice.org	
Netherlands	Dutch government		OpenOffice.org	
South Africa	South African Government			
Spain	Extremadura	gnuLinex (Debian based)	OpenOffice.org	Firefox
Switzerland	Solothurn	Debian	OpenOffice.org	Firefox
Turkey	Ministry of Defense	Pardus	OpenOffice.org	Firefox
USA	Novell	Suse	OpenOffice.org	Firefox
Venezuela	Venezuela government	Canaima (Debian based)	OpenOffice.org	Firefox
Vietnam	IT divisions of government agencies		OpenOffice.org	Firefox

4.3 Productivity of Tested Desktop Solutions

4.3.1 Experiment Subject Profiling

From post-experiment survey, experiment subjects were profiled and their perceptions of both solutions assessed. Following are the graphs profiling the experiment subjects based on the frequency tables from post-experiment survey results listed in Appendix J.

The experiment subjects' genders were categorized as 57.7%

Figure 21: Experiment Subjects' Proficiency According to Gender

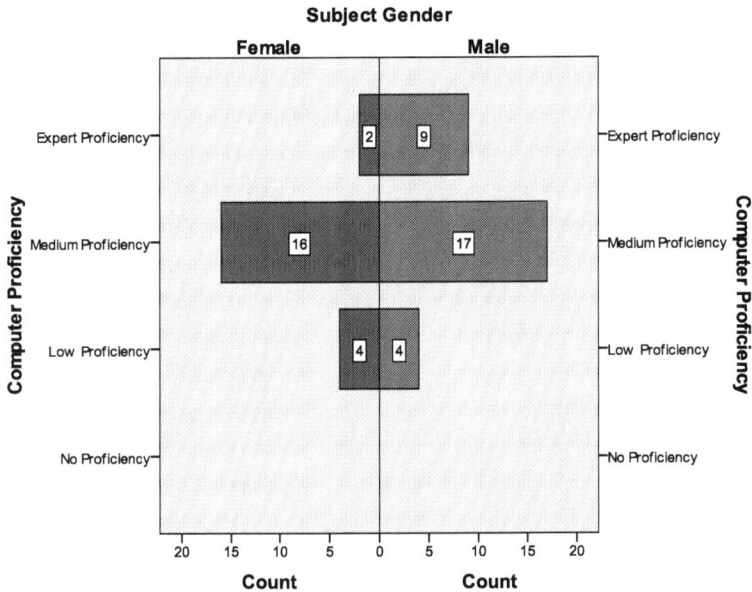

male and 42.3% female. Most respondents (46.2%) fall into the 23-31 years group, 23.1% fall into the 40-48 years group, 17.3% fall into the 32-39 years age group.

In terms of computer proficiency, most subjects (63.5%) categorized themselves in the Medium Proficiency group, while 21.2% placed themselves at Expert Proficiency, and 15.4% in Low Proficiency.

Figure 22: Experiment Subjects' Job Specializations

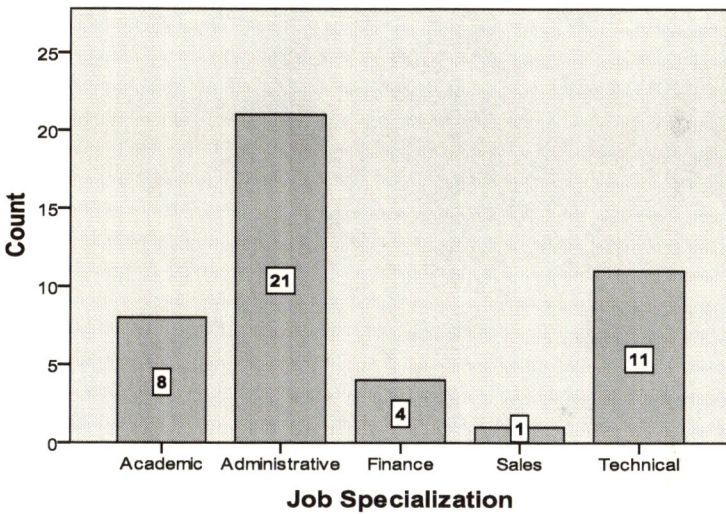

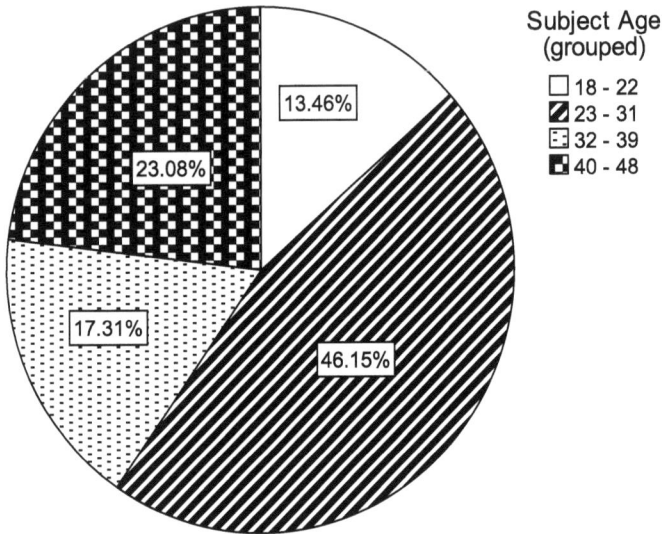

Figure 23: Subject Ratios Per Age Group

Subject Age
(grouped)

☐ 18 - 22
◩ 23 - 31
⊟ 32 - 39
◼ 40 - 48

13.46%

23.08%

17.31%

46.15%

4.3.2   Experiment Timing Analysis: Paired-sample T-test

From the experiment timings in this study, data was gathered in regards to the productivity of experiment subjects as they used two desktop solutions tailored for the organizational environment; one proprietary and the other based on Open Source Software. The Paired-samples T-test analysis resulting from SPSS version 17 software produced the tables on page 121 and 122. From these two tables we can deduce the following:

1. Of the Mean time differences - taken for each of the 8 tasks performed on both Windows Vista and Ubuntu Linux systems -, the Ubuntu Linux system shows a productivity advantage in all tasks, with the exception of tasks 6 and 8.

2. Of all the Mean time differences, the statistical significance in productivity difference measure shows only for tasks 1, 3, and 4 as their Sig value is much lower than 0.05. This is further verified by their 95% confidence interval, which does not contain a 0.

3. The confidence interval results for tasks with a statistically significant difference (1, 3, and 4) give us 95% confidence that the productivity difference advantage for task 1 on Ubuntu Linux lies within the interval between 4.675 and 18.248 seconds, while the productivity difference advantage for task 3 on Ubuntu Linux lies within the interval between 7.260 and 36.010 seconds, and the productivity difference advantage for task 4 on Ubuntu Linux lies within the interval between 3.515 and 16.562 seconds.

4. The Mean time difference of total tasks on Windows Vista versus Ubuntu Linux is statistically significant and shows an overall productivity difference - to the advantage for Ubuntu Linux - which lies within the interval between 17.967 seconds and 1 minute 8.918 seconds for the total tasks.

5. The time difference for total tasks translates into a percentage of productivity increase for users of Ubuntu Linux for these tasks overall. As per the Intel EPMM, calculating for a working week (5 days) with a frequency of 5 per day for the general set of tasks previously listed, the productivity increase is within an interval of 3.02 % to 11.6 % per week compared with the same on Microsoft Windows Vista. The percentage was calculated by dividing each of the lower and upper values of the confidence interval for the "total time for

tasks" pair upon the sum of all "total time for tasks" Means for all experiment subjects.

6. High correlation figures show for the time to perform any of the 8 tasks between the two systems; Windows Vista and Ubuntu Linux, with the exception of tasks 1, and 3.

7. An overall correlation also shows between the total Mean time taken to perform tasks on Windows Vista and the total Mean time to perform the same tasks on the Ubuntu Linux system.

4.3.3 Experiment Subject Perception

On the subject perception part of the survey, 90.4% of Windows Vista users thought it was either "Easy" or "Very Easy" to use the system, and the exact same ratio of users thought the same of Ubuntu Linux.

Of their experience using the Windows Vista system, 73% were either "Satisfied" or "Very Satisfied", while 80.8% of Ubuntu Linux users felt the same of their experience.

Of the post-experiment survey respondents, 67.3% would accept using Windows Vista at work if their organization enforced it, while 63.5% would accept Ubuntu Linux in such a situation. However, 53.8% of all respondents actually preferred Windows Vista for their work environment versus 44.2% who preferred Ubuntu Linux.

Table 3: Paired Samples T-Test

| | | Paired Differences | | | | | | df | Sig. (2-tailed) |
| | Mean | Std. Deviation | Std. Error Mean | 95% Confidence Interval of the Difference | | t | | |
				Lower	Upper			
Pair 1 Vista task 1: Open file from folder - Linux task 1: Open file from folder	0:00:11.462	0:00:24.377	0:00:03.381	0:00:04.675	0:00:18.248	3.390	51	.001
Pair 2 Vista task 2: Print document - Linux task 2: Print document	0:00:04.288	0:00:24.960	0:00:03.461	-0:00:02.660	0:00:11.237	1.239	51	.221
Pair 3 Vista task 3: Save document in folder - Linux task 3: Save document in folder	0:00:21.635	0:00:51.634	0:00:07.160	0:00:07.260	0:00:36.010	3.021	51	.004
Pair 4 Vista task 4: Copy file to folder - Linux task 4: Copy file to folder	0:00:10.038	0:00:23.431	0:00:03.249	0:00:03.515	0:00:16.562	3.089	51	.003
Pair 5 Vista task 5: Format document content then copy - Linux task 5: Format document content then copy	0:00:04.712	0:00:17.855	0:00:02.476	-0:00:00.259	0:00:09.682	1.903	51	.063
Pair 6 Vista task 6: Create document and paste content - Linux task 6: Create document and paste content	-0:00:01.360	0:00:19.636	0:00:02.777	-0:00:06.941	0:00:04.221	-.490	49	.627
Pair 7 Vista task 7: Use Arabic characters to save document - Linux task 7: Use Arabic characters to save document	0:00:03.615	0:00:23.619	0:00:03.275	-0:00:02.960	0:00:10.191	1.104	51	.275
Pair 8 Vista task 8: Attach document to e-mail and send - Linux task 8: Attach document to e-mail and send	-0:00:03.300	0:00:26.414	0:00:03.736	-0:00:10.807	0:00:04.207	-.883	49	.381
Pair 9 Total time for Vista tasks - Total time for Linux tasks	0:00:43.442	0:01:31.506	0:00:12.690	0:00:17.967	0:01:08.918	3.423	51	.001

121

Table 4: Paired Samples Statistics

		Mean	N	Std. Deviation	Std. Error Mean	Correlation
Pair 1	Vista task 1: Open file from folder	0:00:28.404	52	0:00:23.967	0:00:03.324	0.147471148
	Linux task 1: Open file from folder	0:00:16.942	52	0:00:09.221	0:00:01.279	
Pair 2	Vista task 2: Print document	0:00:23.269	52	0:00:22.320	0:00:03.095	0.42490512
	Linux task 2: Print document	0:00:18.981	52	0:00:24.138	0:00:03.347	
Pair 3	Vista task 3: Save document in folder	0:00:53.019	52	0:00:49.595	0:00:06.878	0.165103403
	Linux task 3: Save document in folder	0:00:31.385	52	0:00:24.726	0:00:03.429	
Pair 4	Vista task 4: Copy file to folder	0:00:36.096	52	0:00:32.451	0:00:04.500	0.694512905
	Linux task 4: Copy file to folder	0:00:26.058	52	0:00:24.511	0:00:03.399	
Pair 5	Vista task 5: Format document content then copy	0:00:34.923	52	0:00:24.418	0:00:03.386	0.7322378
	Linux task 5: Format document content then copy	0:00:30.212	52	0:00:24.380	0:00:03.381	
Pair 6	Vista task 6: Create document and paste content	0:00:23.920	50	0:00:19.095	0:00:02.700	0.616676883
	Linux task 6: Create document and paste content	0:00:25.280	50	0:00:24.410	0:00:03.452	
Pair 7	Vista task 7: Use Arabic characters to save document	0:00:35.192	52	0:00:17.948	0:00:02.489	0.407778697
	Linux task 7: Use Arabic characters to save document	0:00:31.577	52	0:00:24.327	0:00:03.374	
Pair 8	Vista task 8: Attach document to e-mail and send	0:00:49.860	50	0:00:25.637	0:00:03.626	0.690611504
	Linux task 8: Attach document to e-mail and send	0:00:53.160	50	0:00:36.519	0:00:05.165	
Pair 9	Total time for Vista tasks	0:04:45.731	52	0:02:15.790	0:00:18.831	0.796606209
	Total time for Linux tasks	0:04:02.288	52	0:02:28.612	0:00:20.609	

Figure 24: Experiment Subjects Perception Ratios

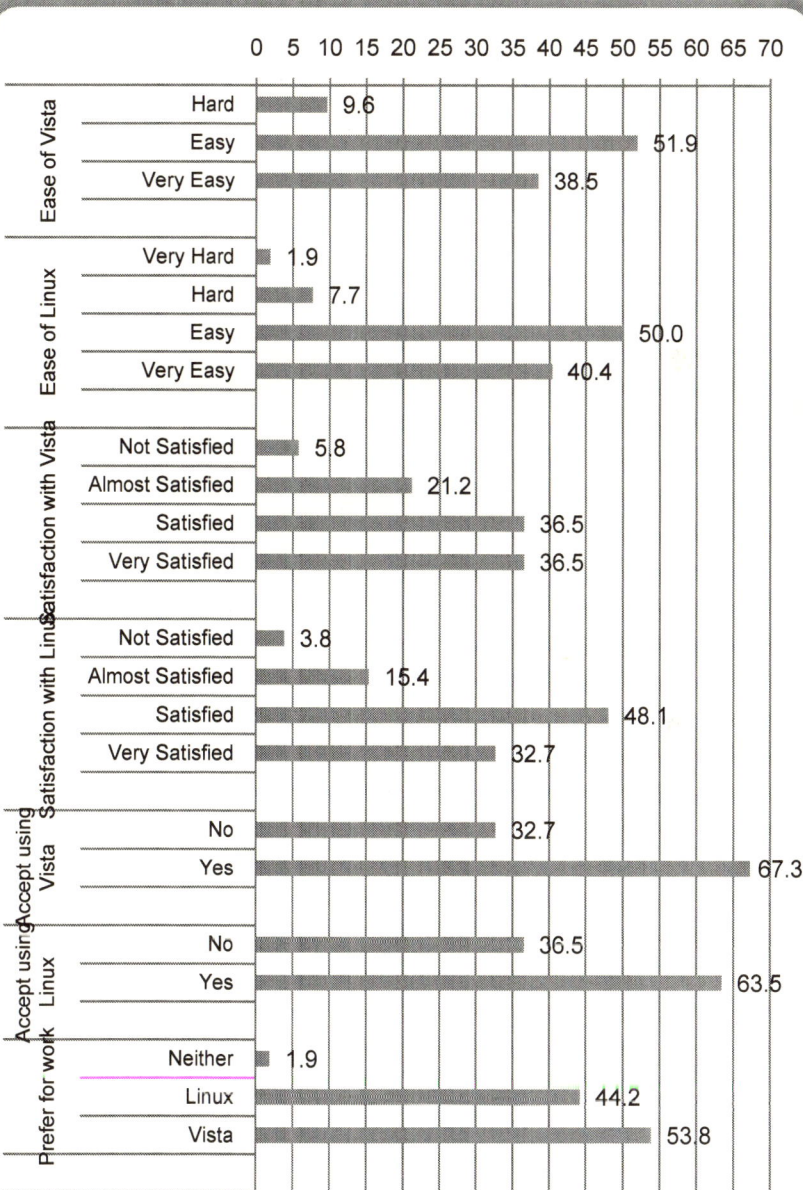

Figure 24: Experiment Subjects Perception Ratios

4.3.4   Experiment Subject Interviews

The interview with experiment subjects revealed the following trends in likes and dislikes of both systems as summarized in the following table:

Table 5: Interview Results for Experiment Subjects

Likes			Dislikes		
	Vista	Linux		Vista	Linux
Easy to use	9	9	Hard to use	6	2
Easy navigation	6	7	Complicated navigation	8	6
Familiar	9	12	Not familiar	7	12
Autocomplete available	3	0	No Autocomplete	0	4
Liked interface	8	5	Interface problems	1	9
Faster	3	15	Slower	7	3
More capable	2	1	Less capable	0	1
Better applications	3	3	Application problems	5	4
			Unstable	1	0

Some Vista users praised the Autocomplete feature and more of them liked the interface in comparison with Linux users. Many more Linux users praised its speed and - to a lesser extent – its familiarity in comparison with Vista users.

In terms of dislikes, some Linux users disliked the missing Autocomplete feature, and many more of them had issues with the interface and - to a lesser extent – its familiarity in comparison with Vista users. While some Vista users complained of its slow performance and complicated usage and -

to a lesser extent - they had more issues with navigation in comparison with Linux users.

5. SUMMARY OF FINDINGS

5.1 Problem Context

The study was launched in order to help organizational decision-makers asses a very specific situation: When contemplating migration to a new proprietary operating system and related applications for organizational desktop computers, what would be the impact on employees' productivity of substituting such a desktop system with Open Source Software alternatives?

5.2   Preliminary Survey Findings

The survey sought to prioritize where the general computing functions of employees lie and what application types are therefore needed. These functions have scientifically been shown as :

1. Printing documents (95.8%)
2. Communicating using e-mail (92.3%)
3. Web browsing (87.3%)
4. Reading PDF documents (83.8%)
5. Reading Arabic documents (79.6%)
6. Accessing documents on a server through the organization's network (55.6%)
7. Uses a word-processing application (43.7%)
8. Producing spreadsheets (33.8%)
9. Using the Microsoft Office suite of applications (22.5%)
10. Calendaring and scheduling (19%)
11. Using software to create presentations (18.3%)

The main software required for the above functions falls within three types:

1. Operating system
2. Office-like suite of applications
3. Web browser

Some findings not directly related to this study can also be deduced:

- E-mail communication has caught the work place and cemented its position well. Yet reliance on the printed document workflow is still very strong as well in the Arabic region.

- The Internet with its vast knowledge base and the trend towards web-based applications has become a necessary part of the work place.

- Readers of documents are nearly double the number of writers and editors. Collaboration may not be in high usage in such a case.

- The use of organizer software for group/individual calendaring and scheduling only starting to appear on the region's horizon.

5.3 Research Findings

Research was conducted in order to find the best suited software for the previous three software types required for this study's experiment.

For operating systems, an abundant choice was available, Ubuntu, Suse, and Fedora are all of close proximity in features and supportability. Ubuntu was chosen for its desktop focus and widest community adoption.

For the application suite, OpenOffice.org is by far the best supported with no clear competition in sight. It has the best development record with a steady cycle of fixes and features constantly being introduced.

For the web browser, while many browsers are in active use and development, Firefox – like OpenOffice.org - leads by far in technological features, user satisfaction, and community adoption.

Most successful organizational desktop migrations worldwide have diversified in their choice of operating system (Linux distribution), but have always relied on OpenOffice.org and Firefox as part of their plans. Oddly, most of these migrations – rather than choosing a company-supported distribution - relied on in-house Linux expertise, and chose the Debian project, a derivative, or their own Debian customization. Debian is known for being very modular and customizable. But their choice also seems to be built on Debian having the widest development community and the most diversified set of software packages while maintaining excellent project administration for a very lengthy track record. Ubuntu is also a Debian derivative.

The study of those worldwide OSS migration scenarios also depicts the close proximity of organizational needs for the same software types globally in today's organizational culture. It more importantly emphasizes the OSS solution's ability to cater for the widely varying language needs of different countries' cultures and populations.

Some findings not directly related to this study can also be deduced:

- Linux desktop usage has been rising slowly but steadily for years. But 2009 has been the year marking desktop

Linux's first reach of the 1% market share in used installations.

- Some online usage surveys – such as W3Counter - already place Linux at above 2% of the installed base share.

- The large difference in satisfaction between Firefox and Internet Explorer - while the latter still holds the largest market share - is attributed to IE being installed by default on all Windows machines. Some analysts have interpreted this as a condition stemming from users who use the default browser in their work environment while choosing Firefox for their home computer usage.

5.4 Experiment Findings

An experiment was performed to record the timing of a set of tasks for the same group of users on both the Windows Vista and the Ubuntu Linux desktop solutions, which had been created with an organizational objective within their design.

The purpose was to arrive at the productivity of each solution based on the Intel EPMM model with some modifications towards measurement enhancement by implementing a Paired-sample T-test analysis.

The analysis has shown a significant difference in employee productivity between the two solutions to the advantage of Ubuntu Linux. The advantage lies in an interval of 3.02 % to 11.6 % increase in productivity within a 5-day working week and a frequency of 5 executions per day for the general set of tasks previously listed compared with the same on the Microsoft Windows Vista system.

The mentioned set of general tasks includes: navigating folders, copying and opening files, creating, saving and printing documents, copying and pasting content, and communicating via e-mail.

The productivity advantage is strongest in folder navigation aspects, including locating, copying, and saving files.

There is a clear correlation between users' performance of tasks on Windows Vista and Ubuntu Linux, leading to the conclusion that skills gained on one system will pay-off as an advantage for the user migrated to the other system.

Unlike Windows Vista, the customization of the Linux distribution's user interface is much more thorough and easily accessible. The complete "look and feel" can be completely transformed to suit the organization's users and needs quite easily.

Some findings not directly related to this study can also be deduced:

- Virtualization has proved its cost saving ability and advantages in creating multiple identical test environments through its many facets and features. VirtualBox is an excellent OSS example of this concept as seen through its intensive use throughout this study.

5.5   Observation Findings

Some findings from observation of the experiment subjects follow:

- The Ubuntu Linux interface got more favorable response from users after installing a theme resembling Mac OS X and background wallpaper resembling Windows Xp.

- Subjects were more eager to have introductory time with Linux than with Vista. The name Windows alone seems to suggest familiarity, but after the experiment, most agree to Linux actually being more familiar. Most of the unfamiliarity in the Vista solution stems from the new Office 2007 "ribbon" interface and the Windows Explorer interface changes.

- The performance differences between the two solutions were obvious in the responsiveness of Linux versus Windows Vista. The overhead showed most especially when running an Office 2007 application such as Word on top of the already tasked Windows Vista environment, where saving would cause a temporary – but relatively lengthy - non-responsive situation in most cases.

5.6   Post-Experiment Survey and Interview Findings

The higher satisfaction rate of Linux users compared to Windows Vista in the post experiment survey came as a surprise to the researcher. It prompted much investigation into the reasons behind such ratings, which the interviews with experiment subjects had easily helped uncover.

In trying to diversify reasons for upgrade, one of the strategies deployed by Microsoft for increasing both Windows Vista and Office 2007 adoption was to put both through a complete interface overhaul in comparison to their predecessors. This has prompted users to speak out against the need to re-learn their normal workflows which they had become accustomed to. User agitation shows in the higher number of users who labeled Vista as "hard to use", and the slightly higher number of "harder to navigate" complaints. Many also complained of Vista's unfamiliarity or praised the familiar workflow provided by Ubuntu Linux.

Windows Vista's performance also lacked and caused user frustration. This is mainly due to the higher minimum memory requirements of 1 GB. Meanwhile, Linux worked smoothly with its minimum memory requirements which do not exceed 256 MB.

Still, most users noticed Vista's prettier interface. But it seems that looks alone did not do enough to sway user satisfaction to Vista's side. On the other hand, features like Autocomplete were missed by some in Ubuntu Linux's applications.

An estimated two-thirds of respondents were willing to work with whatever their organization chose for their desktops. Only a small margin (9.6%) preferred Vista for use at work, most probably due to their fear of lack in capability or compatibility.

5.7 Study Limitations

5.7.1 General Use

As the study attempted to gather and test from the very start only the most generally used organizational desktop computer functions, its results will only accurately describe a "general use" situation as described and practiced throughout this study.

Any attempt to gain the same results of this study for more specific areas of desktop computing - whether inside or outside the boundaries of an organization – would not be supportable through this study alone. This pertains to areas such as desktop publishing, multimedia authoring, software development, engineering graphics, game play, and educational use. Whether these special areas render a better or worse productivity result would have to be studied separately.

5.7.2 Software Currency

In the current situation, Microsoft Corporation plans to launch the next version of its Windows operating system – referred to as Windows 7 – within 2009 (Protalinski, 2009), three years after launching its Vista operating system. The next version of Microsoft Office – codenamed Office 14 – is planned for release in 2010 (Lai, 2009), around 4 years after the previously released version; Office 2007 (Hill, 2006). Meanwhile, innovators in the Open Source community have been pushing their technologies forward at a more rapid pace, with new features officially released every six months, as in the case of the Ubuntu Linux distribution (Shuttleworth, 2008) and the current OpenOffice.org release cycle (Siddall, 2006).

As in any information technology subject, this study along with its research, experiments, and surveys, is dependent on the technologies currently available in the software market. As these technologies change – for both proprietary and Open Source solutions – the results will need to be revisited and re-evaluated, and new findings accordingly published. It is fair to say - in such a case - that an annual re-evaluation of the subject matter of this study, based on newly released products and technologies to the desktop computer software market, is quite appropriate - and even required - in order that the results are continually validated.

5.7.3 Confidence Interval

The study, more time permitting, could have lowered the confidence interval to 8 if it had raised the number of experiment subjects to 150. But due to the time and resource constraints, no more than 52 subjects were used in the experiment, leading to a confidence interval of 13.6.

5.7.4 Experiment Bias

As previously stated on page 86: "The decision to start with the Windows platform was in order to level the handicaps between the two scenarios. If we start with Windows, the subjects will be in an environment they are more accustomed with, handling the challenge of familiarizing themselves with the test script. When the subjects are given the Linux environment, they will have accustomed themselves to the test script but faced with the new challenge of familiarizing themselves with Linux. If we had started with Linux, the subjects would have had the double challenge of familiarizing themselves with both the new test script as well as the new computing environment.

There may be a perceived bias in this scenario towards the Linux system, as it is where the user ran the tasks last. This could be countered- balanced by the psychological familiarity of the Windows brand name and its ties to perceived features, compatibility, and ease of use.

The question still stands as to whether or not the biases on both sides truly negate each other in order to ultimately render a non-biased experiment result. This is an unresolved issue, which may be an inherent fault in the Intel methodology and is therefore worthy of further research as mentioned in 6.3.2 of Recommendations for Further Research on page 143.

Nevertheless, this point does not negate the ease of which OSS solutions can be adapted to by organizational employees with little to no extra time and cost when the solutions are well planned and designed to do so.

6. CONCLUSION AND RECOMMENDATIONS

6.1 Study Results

The study has achieved all of its stated objectives, and - through them - has uncovered much relative information in its area of concern. It has also touched on aspects of employee psychology and software migration methodology.

There is a very close resemblance between regional organizations' specific needs from employee desktop computers and those of other organizations worldwide.

Proprietary software development in its most current state today – specifically, Microsoft Windows Vista - is not properly targeting an increase in user productivity in the short-term. Neither is it achieving higher user satisfaction in the short-term.

Today's OSS solutions constitute a mature alternative desktop tool for general employee productivity in the work environment.

The customization capabilities of OSS solutions include the wide range of available language localizations as well as the flexibility to adapt to an organization's cultural norms.

The Intel Employee Productivity Measure Methodology is a sound and practical methodology when coupled with knowledge of its drawbacks and how to counter them. Some of these drawbacks were uncovered in detail through this study.

Quantitative statistical analysis proves the additional productivity benefits of OSS desktop solutions to organizations versus the Microsoft Windows Vista proprietary solution in the short-term.

Correlation shows that employees' learned skills are leveraged between desktop computer systems - and not reset - when migrating from proprietary to Open Source desktop solutions.

Coupled with a proven lower long-term TCO, an OSS desktop solutions' productivity is an additional value to the strategic IT planning objectives of the CIO or IT decision-maker of any organization and goes beyond what proprietary desktop software offers today.

A call to action for the software development community and software development organizations as the study points to the market leaders in desktop OSS projects; The momentum gained by these valuable desktop solutions can be further accelerated, and the value produced by them can be further enhanced by adding more contributions to their open community projects. The returns will - in turn - affect all market players, and present a common ground usable by all parties to further technological software development and evolution.

6.2 Study Contribution

The study has contributed in the following concerned areas:

6.2.1 Target Audience

To the Information Technology decision-maker, this study has:

- Uncovered the most common organizational desktop computer functions as well as the best OSS alternatives to satisfy those requirements.
- Provided an insight into a scientific, refined, and practical methodology to perform employee productivity benchmarking in the IT field for both software and hardware solutions.
- Provided a cross-platform utility for the Intel EPMM; a necessary software benchmarking tool I have called "Intaj".
- Provided a relevant and timely answer to the employee productivity variable when evaluating proprietary versus Open Source software solutions.
- The study aids decision-makers in making decisions that usually cost organizations a considerable amount of their budgets each year in terms of software licensing, maintenance, and support.
- The study has detailed how an organizational OSS solution can be built, customized, and localized.
- Successful worldwide migration scenarios have been researched and gathered in this study in order to help as

a template for organizational migration to desktop OSS solutions.

- The study provided feedback from the field on what an organization's management can expect as a short-term reaction from employees in the case of endeavoring to migrate their desktop computer software to OSS alternatives.

6.2.2 Scientific Research

To the scientific community in general, a practical implementation of the Intel EPMM process on two software solutions has been provided through this study. Further, some drawbacks in the Intel methodology have been highlighted through my critique of the Intel EPMM.

To the computer science community, a refined methodology has been introduced that can serve in evaluating the productivity variable of future software solution developments.

To the management sciences community, I have introduced the Open Source movement and its objectives.

Also, as much had been done in past research to highlight the aspects of Open Source server software. Today, a study has brought light upon the desktop (client) aspects of Open Source software development.

The study has further detailed how evaluation of at least one aspect of software solutions – and a very critical one when it comes to productivity – can practically take place.

To the software development community, an additional scope of user viewpoint and feedback has been introduced, in regards to both the latest proprietary and Open Source solutions and the organizational employee's demands from them.

The study also provides directive to those software developers and software development organizations who would like to contribute to the Open Source movement by guiding them towards the OSS market leaders where their efforts can benefit the general community most and fastest.

6.3   Recommendations for Further Research

I recommend the following aspects to be further studied in the near future, whether by Master or PhD thesis students.

6.3.1   Lower Confidence Interval

The study, more time and resources permitting, could have lowered the confidence interval to 8 if it had raised the number of experiment subjects to 150. But due to the time and resource constraints, no more than 52 subjects were used in the experiment, leading to a confidence interval of 13.6.

6.3.2   The Benchmarking Model

Parts of the Intel EPMM model have already been criticized in this study as in 2.3.5 Drawbacks of Intel's Methodology on page 63. The model could be further enhanced with additional research into where its limits and drawbacks lie and how to counter such negative scenarios.

6.3.3   Long-Term Effects

As the study experimented within the Bahraini community, which currently has no visible long-term Open Source software implementations – and hence the need for this study's experiment –, a study of the long-term effects of Open Source desktop software on employee productivity would definitely produce more viable results and render a more realistic picture of the issue.

6.3.4   Further Organizational Concerns

As productivity is but a single variable of many to be considered by decision makers before deeming Open Source desktop software to be truly feasible for organizational implementation, there are many other aspects of this type of software yet to be fully studied and understood, including: employee perception and trainability, manageability, performance, compatibility, security, supportability, cost-effectiveness, ROI, TCO, development cycle, licensing models, as well as many other aspects of desktop OSS for organizations.

This is most especially relevant for those aspects that directly affect productivity, such as:

- Security, through lesser virus attacks or user mishaps.
- Manageability, as lack of user acquaintance with non-work related programs keeps employees focused on work-related tasks.
- Compatibility, in order to serve a wider application portfolio to a wider employee range.

6.3.5   Specific Usage Areas

Productivity of proprietary versus Open Source software can be studied under less generalized usage conditions for valid results within more specific scenarios. Such areas of desktop computer usage include desktop publishing, multimedia authoring, software development, engineering graphics, game play, and educational use.

تمت بحمد الله

Finished by Allah's Grace

BIBLIOGRAPHY

Acohido, Byron. 2003. Linux took on Microsoft, and won big in Munich. *usatoday.com.* [Online] July 17, 2003. [Cited: April 4, 2009.]
http://www.usatoday.com/money/industries/technology/2003-07-13-microsoft-linux-munich_x.htm.

Berlind, David. 2007. Trouble in Vista paradise? Large software vendor warns of major compatibility problems and burdensome remedies. *ZDNet.com.* [Online] CBS Interactive Inc., January 25, 2007. [Cited: February 19, 2009.]
http://blogs.zdnet.com/Berlind/?p=315.

Bierhals, Gregor. 2009. Towards the freedom of the operating system: the French Gendarmerie goes for Ubuntu . *Open Source Observatory and Repository.* [Online] European Commision, February 25, 2009. [Cited: April 6, 2009.]
http://www.osor.eu/case_studies/towards-the-freedom-of-the-operating-system-the-french-gendarmerie-goes-for-ubuntu.

Blanco, Elena. 2009. Open source and the web browser. *oss-watch.ac.uk.* [Online] University of Oxford, May 6, 2009. [Cited: June 7, 2009.] http://www.oss-watch.ac.uk/resources/webbrowser.xml.

Bodnar, Ladislav. 2009. Linux Distributions - Facts and Figures. *DistroWatch.com.* [Online] DistroWatch.com, June 7, 2009. [Cited: June 7, 2009.]
http://distrowatch.com/stats.php?section=popularity.

Brown, Carol V., et al. 2009. *Managing Information Technology.* s.l. : Pearson Prentice Hall, 2009. 978-0-13-814661-0.

Business Readiness Rating. 2006. GRAM BRR. *Business Readiness Rating.* [Online] Business Readiness Rating, March 28, 2006. [Cited: June 7, 2009.]
http://www.openbrr.org/wiki/index.php/GRAM_BRR.

Cabello, Percy. 2007. Opera's Speed Dial for Firefox. *Mozilla Links.* [Online] Mozilla Links, April 27, 2007. [Cited: March 22,

2009.] http://mozillalinks.org/wp/2007/04/operas-speed-dial-for-firefox/.

Calbet, Xavier. 2005. Forget Munich's Linux Migration, It's Already Done by Extremadura. *OSnews.com.* [Online] OSNews LLC, November 10, 2005. [Cited: April 3, 2009.] http://www.osnews.com/story/12611.

Cooper, Danese, et al. 2006. Open Sources 2.0. *O'Reilly Commons.* [Online] 2006. [Cited: March 5, 2009.] http://commons.oreilly.com/wiki/index.php/Open_Sources_26T.

Creative Research Systems. 2009. Sample Size Calculator. *Creative Research Systems.* [Online] Creative Research Systems, 2009. [Cited: May 16, 2009.] http://www.surveysystem.com/sscalc.htm.

Cybersource® Pty. Ltd. 2004. Linux vs. Windows. *Cybersource.* [Online] Cybersource, December 13, 2004. [Cited: February 15, 2009.] http://www.cyber.com.au/cyber/about/linux_vs_windows_tco_comparison.pdf.

Desktop Linux. 2007. 2007 Desktop Linux Market survey. *Desktop Linux.* [Online] Ziff Davis Enterprise Holdings Inc., August 21, 2007. [Cited: June 12, 2009.] http://www.desktoplinux.com/cgi-bin/survey/survey.cgi?view=archive&id=0813200712407.

Dolezal, Vlad. 2008. Why Linux Doesn't Spread - the Curse of Being Free. *An Amazing Mind.* [Online] Vlad Dolezal, February 16, 2008. [Cited: February 20, 2009.] http://anamazingmind.com/blog/2008/why-linux-doesnt-spread-the-curse-of-being-free/.

Dotzler, Asa. 2009. how many linux users are there. *Asa Dotzler: Firefox and more.* [Online] weblogs.mozillazine.org, February 18, 2009. [Cited: February 20, 2009.] http://weblogs.mozillazine.org/asa/archives/2009/02/how_many_linux.html.

—. **2005.** Why Linux isn't ready for desktops. *ZDNet Australia.* [Online] CBS Interactive, July 18, 2005. [Cited: February 20,

2009.] http://www.zdnet.com.au/news/software/soa/Why-Linux-isn-t-ready-for-desktops/0,130061733,139202374,00.htm.

Flor., Ivan Muela. 2008. Ecuador migrates to Free Software and Open Standards. *Digital Standards Organization.* [Online] April 11, 2008. [Cited: April 4, 2009.] http://www.digistan.org/forum/t-52909/ecuador-migrates-to-free-software-and-open-standards.

gHacks.net. 2009. Web Browser Popularity. *gHacks.net.* [Online] gHacks.net, March 21, 2009. [Cited: March 22, 2009.] http://www.ghacks.net/2009/03/21/web-browser-popularity/.

Gillar, Johannes. 2004. Matthias Vering on Usability and User Productivity. *SAP Design Guild.* [Online] SAP AG, November 19, 2004. [Cited: March 13, 2009.] http://www.sapdesignguild.org/editions/edition8/leading_article.asp.

GITOC. 2007. Government embraces open source. *GITOC OSS site.* [Online] GITOC OSS site, February 26, 2007. [Cited: March 28, 2009.] http://www.oss.gov.za/modules.php?op=modload&name=News&file=article&sid=151&mode=thread&order=0&thold=0.

Gralla, Preston. 2007. More Reasons Why Linux Will Never Take Over the Desktop. *O'Reilly WindowsDevCenter Blog.* [Online] O'Reilly Media, Inc., April 25, 2007. [Cited: February 20, 2009.] http://www.oreillynet.com/windows/blog/2007/04/more_reasons_why_linux_will_ne_3.html.

Gray, James. 2009. Readers' Choice Awards 2009. *Linux Journal.* [Online] Linux Journal, June 1, 2009. [Cited: June 12, 2009.] http://www.linuxjournal.com/article/10451.

Griffith, Arthur. 2007. *SPSS for Dummies.* s.l. : Wiley Publishing, 2007. 978-0-470-11344-8.

Hadfield, Will. 2005. Cost of abandoning Windows too great for Linux Desktop migration. *computerweekly.com.* [Online] Reed Business Information Ltd., August 10, 2005. [Cited: March 29, 2009.]

http://www.computerweekly.com/Articles/2005/08/10/211333/cost-of-abandoning-windows-too-great-for-linux-desktop.htm.

Hill, Brandon. 2006. Vista, Office 2007 Now Available for Volume Licensing. *Dailytech.com.* [Online] DailyTech LLC., December 1, 2006. [Cited: June 6, 2009.] http://www.dailytech.com/article.aspx?newsid=5165.

Hillenius, Gijs. 2009. Foreign ministry: 'Cost of Open Source desktop maintenance is by far the lowest' . *Open Source Observatory.* [Online] European Commission, January 20, 2009. [Cited: April 6, 2009.] http://www.osor.eu/news/de-foreign-ministry-cost-of-open-source-desktop-maintenance-is-by-far-the-lowest.

—. **2008.** Half of all desktop PCs at ministry of Justice migrated to GNU/Linux . *OSOR.EU.* [Online] Open Source Observatory, October 1, 2008. [Cited: April 7, 2009.] http://www.osor.eu/news/be-half-of-all-desktop-pcs-ministry-of-justice-migrated-to-gnu-linux.

Hoffer, Jeffrey A., George, Joey F. and Valacich, Joseph S. 2008. *Modern Systems Analysis and Design.* s.l. : Pearson Prentice Hall, 2008. 0-13-613-296-0.

Intel Corporation. 2004. *Measuring Employee Productivity: Data collection and analysis methods for productivity studies at Intel.* [PDF] s.l. : Intel, 2004.

—. **2003.** *Putting a Value on Productivity: Measuring IT-enhanced employee.* s.l. : Intel Corporation, 2003.

Jackson, Randal. 2007. AA dumps Open Office, buys Microsoft for 'compatibility'. *Computerworld.* [Online] Fairfax Business Group , July 16, 2007. [Cited: February 20, 2009.] http://computerworld.co.nz/news.nsf/tech/A6AB17B34B1BA81ECC2573160079BFBC.

Kanellos, Michael. 2002. PCs: More than 1 billion served. *CNET News.* [Online] CBS Interactive Inc., June 30, 2002. [Cited: February 11, 2009.] http://news.cnet.com/2100-1040-940713.html.

Keizer, Gregg. 2008. Windows market share dives below 90% for first time. *Computerworld.* [Online] International Data Group Inc., December 1, 2008. [Cited: February 11, 2009.] http://www.computerworld.com/action/article.do?command=view ArticleBasic&articleId=9121938.

Knowledge@Wharton. 2007. Rivals Set Their Sights on Microsoft Office: Can They Topple the Giant? *Knowledge@Wharton.* [Online] Knowledge@Wharton, August 22, 2007. [Cited: February 15, 2009.] http://knowledge.wharton.upenn.edu/article.cfm?articleid=1795.

Kolawa, Adam. 2008. How Better Software Can Save the World. *www.cio.com.* [Online] CXO Media Inc. An International Data Group(IDG) Company, October 10, 2008. [Cited: March 10, 2009.] http://www.cio.com/article/454215/How_Better_Software_Can_S ave_the_World?page=1.

Lai, Eric. 2009. Microsoft: Office 14 won't ship until 2010. *Computerworld.com.* [Online] International Data Group Inc. , February 24, 2009. [Cited: June 6, 2009.] http://www.computerworld.com/action/article.do?command=view ArticleBasic&articleId=9128541.

Linux Counter. 2009. Linux Counter Machine Report. *Linux Counter.* [Online] Linux Counter, June 12, 2009. [Cited: June 12, 2009.] http://counter.li.org/reports/machines.php.

Lowe, Scott. 2009. Macs Rarely Belong in the Enterprise. *CIO Web site.* [Online] CXO Media Inc., February 23, 2009. [Cited: February 27, 2009.] http://www.cio.com/article/481880/Macs_Rarely_Belong_in_the_ Enterprise.

Malaysian Public Sector OSS Portal . 2009. Malaysian Public Sector OSS Portal . *Malaysian Public Sector OSS Portal .* [Online] March 31, 2009. [Cited: April 4, 2009.] http://www.oscc.org.my/.

Microsoft Corp. . 2007. Measuring Performance in Windows Vista. *Microsoft.com.* [Online] July 2, 2007. [Cited: March 5,

2009.]
http://www.microsoft.com/whdc/system/sysperf/Vista_perf.mspx.

Microsoft Corporation. 2009. 2007 Microsoft Office system
requirements. *Microsoft Office Online.* [Online] Microsoft
Corporation, 2009. [Cited: February 18, 2009.]
http://office.microsoft.com/en-us/help/HA101668651033.aspx.

—. **2009.** Microsoft Support Lifecycle. *Microsoft Help and
Support.* [Online] Microsoft Corporation, 2009. [Cited: February
19, 2009.] http://support.microsoft.com/lifecycle/?p1=3223.

—. System requirements. *Get Windows Vista.* [Online] Microsoft
Corporation. [Cited: February 19, 2009.]
http://www.microsoft.com/windows/windows-vista/get/system-
requirements.aspx.

Ministry of Economic Affairs. 2007. *The Netherlands in Open
Connection.* [PDF] The Hague : Ministry of Economic Affairs,
Netherlands, 2007.

Munich Linux Watch. 2009. Munich Linux Watch. *Munich Linux
Watch.* [Online] January 2009. [Cited: April 3, 2009.]
http://limuxwatch.blogspot.com/2008/01/timeline-of-failure.html.

Municipality of Munich. 2008. LiMux - Die IT-Evolution.
muenechen.de. [Online] November 2008. [Cited: April 3, 2009.]
http://www.muenchen.de/Rathaus/dir/limux/publ/147183/index.ht
ml.

Net Applications. 2009. OS market share. *Market Share.*
[Online] Net Applications, February 10, 2009. [Cited: February
11, 2009.] http://marketshare.hitslink.com/os-market-
share.aspx?qprid=9.

Nielson, Gary. 2008. Three reasons Linux can't take over the
desktop. *GaryNielson.com.* [Online] GaryNielson.com, August
23, 2008. [Cited: February 20, 2009.]
http://garynielson.wordpress.com/2008/08/23/three-reasons-
linux-cant-take-over-the-desktop/.

northxsouth. 2008. Protecting sovereignty with free software is
a good idea and the duty of governments, says Stallman. *Free

Software in Latin America. [Online] November 18, 2008. [Cited: April 4, 2009.] http://news.northxsouth.com/2008/11/18/protecting-sovereignty-with-free-software-is-a-good-idea-and-the-duty-of-governments-says-stallman/.

Novell Inc. 2004. The Novell Migration to Linux. [Online] 2004. [Cited: April 19, 2009.] http://www.dell.com/downloads/global/solutions/novell_migration.pdf.

Observatory, Open Source. 2008. Solothurn canton migrates desktops to Open Source. *Open Source Observatory.* [Online] European Commission, May 28, 2008. [Cited: April 7, 2009.] http://www.osor.eu/news/ch-solothurn-canton-migrates-desktops-to-open.

Open Source Observatory and Repository. 2008. First two public institutes switch to Open Source desktop. *Open Source Observatory and Repository.* [Online] European Commission, May 28, 2008. [Cited: April 18, 2009.] http://www.osor.eu/news/nl-first-two-public-institutes-switch-to-open.

—. **2008.** Parliament selects Ubuntu Linux for desktop . *Open Source Observatory and Repository.* [Online] European Commission, May 28, 2008. [Cited: April 17, 2009.] http://www.osor.eu/news/fr-parliament-selects-ubuntu-linux-for-desktop.

OpenOffice.org. 2009. OpenOffice.org Statistics. *OpenOffice.org.* [Online] Sun Microsystems, Inc., June 12, 2009. [Cited: June 12, 2009.] http://stats.openoffice.org/index.html.

Protalinski, Emil. 2008. Microsoft Office 14 to arrive late 2009/early 2010. *Ars Technica.* [Online] Condé Nast Digital, July 30, 2008. [Cited: February 20, 2009.] http://arstechnica.com/microsoft/news/2008/07/microsoft-office-14-to-arrive-late-2009early-2010.ars.

—. **2009.** More proof that Microsoft wants Windows 7 out in 2009. *Ars Technica.* [Online] Condé Nast Digital, January 31, 2009. [Cited: February 20, 2009.]

http://arstechnica.com/microsoft/news/2009/01/more-proof-that-microsoft-wants-windows-7-out-in-2009.ars.

Raymond, Eric Steven. 2000. A Brief History of Hackerdom. *Thyrsus Enterprises.* [Online] August 25, 2000. [Cited: March 5, 2009.] http://www.tuxedo.org/~esr/.

—. **2002.** Afterword: Beyond Software? *http://www.tuxedo.org/~esr/.* [Online] August 2, 2002. [Cited: March 5, 2009.] http://www.tuxedo.org/~esr/.

—. **2000.** Revenge of the Hackers. *http://www.tuxedo.org/~esr/.* [Online] August 26, 2000. [Cited: March 5, 2009.] http://www.tuxedo.org/~esr/.

—. **1998.** The Cathedral and The Bazaar. *Free-soft.org.* [Online] November 22, 1998. [Cited: March 4, 2009.] http://www.free-soft.org/literature/papers/esr/cathedral-bazaar/.

Riley, David D. 2006. *The Object of Java.* s.l. : Pearson Education, 2006. 0-321-33158-3.

Rio, Josep del. 2009. Speed Dial Version History. *Firefox Add-ons.* [Online] Mozilla, January 23, 2009. [Cited: March 22, 2009.] https://addons.mozilla.org/en-US/firefox/addons/versions/4810.

Robert Frances Group, Inc. 2002. Total Cost of Ownership for Linux in the Enterprise. *Linux & IBM.* [Online] IBM, July 2002. [Cited: February 15, 2009.] http://www-03.ibm.com/linux/RFG-LinuxTCO-vFINAL-Jul2002.pdf.

Rosenberg, Donald K. 2000 . Open Source: The Unauthorized White Papers. *Stromian.com.* [Online] 2000 . [Cited: March 4, 2009.] http://www.stromian.com/Book/Chap1.html6T. 0-7645-4660-0.

Sauro, Jeff and Dumas, Joe. 2008. Measuring User Productivity. *Usable Apps Blog.* [Online] blogs.oracle.com, June 13, 2008. [Cited: March 13, 2009.] http://blogs.oracle.com/usableapps//2008/06/measuring_user_productivity.html.

Schreyer, Paul. 2001. Measuring Productivity. *www.sourceoecd.com.* [Online] 2001. [Cited: March 14, 2009.] www.sourceoecd.com.

Scott, Brendan. 2002. Why Free Software's Long Run TCO must be lower. *Brendan Scott's Website.* [Online] July 16, 2002. [Cited: February 15, 2009.] http://www.members.optushome.com.au/brendanscott/papers/freesoftwaretco150702.html.

Shuttleworth, Mark. 2008. The Art of Release. *Mark Shuttleworth.* [Online] Mark Shuttleworth, May 12, 2008. [Cited: February 20, 2009.] http://www.markshuttleworth.com/archives/146.

Siddall, Clytie. 2006. Proposal: changes to the release model. *The Mail Archive.* [Online] The Mail Archive, November 30, 2006. [Cited: February 20, 2009.] http://www.mail-archive.com/releases@openoffice.org/msg01974.html.

Smith, David Mitchell, et al. 2003. Linux on the Desktop: The Whole Story. *Gartner Research.* [Online] Gartner, Inc., August 8, 2003. [Cited: February 20, 2009.] http://www.gartner.com/DisplayDocument?id=406459.

Sowe, Sulayman K. 2008. A new kid on the block. *Open Source Observatory and Repository .* [Online] European Commission, November 27, 2008. [Cited: April 6, 2009.] http://www.osor.eu/case_studies/a-new-kid-on-the-block-the-turkish-pardus-linux-distribution.

Stallman, Richard. 2008. About the GNU Project. *The GNU Project.* [Online] Free Software Foundation, January 21, 2008. [Cited: February 19, 2009.] http://www.gnu.org/gnu/the-gnu-project.html.

—. 2008. About the GNU Project. *GNU Project.* [Online] January 21, 2008. [Cited: March 4, 2009.] http://www.gnu.org/gnu/thegnuproject.html.

—. 1999. Copyleft: Pragmatic Idealism. *GNU Project.* [Online] February 1, 1999. [Cited: March 5, 2009.] http://www.free-soft.org/literature/papers/gnu/pragmatic.html.

—. **1998.** The GNU Manifesto. *GNU Project.* [Online] December 17, 1998. [Cited: March 4, 2009.] http://www.free-soft.org/literature/papers/gnu/manifesto.html.

SurveyWare. 2009. Which is the best browser? *SurveyWare.* [Online] Net Apps, June 12, 2009. [Cited: June 12, 2009.] http://www.surveyware.com/report.aspx?qprid=1&qpnoauth=1&qps=1&qpcustomc=99&qpcustom=595.

Swigart, Scott and Campbell, Sean. 2008. Interview with Warren Woodford - Founder of Mepis. *How Software is Built.* [Online] How Software is Built, December 12, 2008. [Cited: February 20, 2009.] http://howsoftwareisbuilt.com/2008/12/12/interview-with-warren-woodford-founder-of-mepis/#corporate.

Sylvester, IdaRose. 2008. The price of free. *Freeform Comment.* [Online] www.freeformdynamics.com, November 12, 2008. [Cited: February 19, 2009.] http://freeformcomment.blogspot.com/2008/11/price-of-free.html.

Tan, Aaron. 2007. India's Kerala state goes open source. *ZDNet.com.* [Online] CBS Interactive Inc., June 29, 2007. [Cited: April 18, 2009.] http://news.zdnet.com/2100-3513_22-152441.html.

The Linux Counter. 2009. The Linux Counter. *The Linux Counter.* [Online] The Linux Counter, February 20, 2009. [Cited: February 20, 2009.] http://counter.li.org/.

Thurston, Richard. 2007. Cuba gripped by open source fever. *silicon.com.* [Online] CBS Interactive Limited, February 19, 2007. [Cited: March 28, 2009.] http://software.silicon.com/os/0,39024651,39165862,00.htm.

Trochim, William M.K. 2006. The T-Test. *Research Methods Knowledge Base.* [Online] William M K Trochim, October 20, 2006. [Cited: June 13, 2009.] http://www.socialresearchmethods.net/kb/stat_t.php.

U.S. Bureau of Labor Statistics. ILC Frequently Asked Questions. *http://stats.bls.gov.* [Online] U.S. Department of

Labor. [Cited: March 11, 2009.]
http://stats.bls.gov/fls/flsfaqs.htm#Whatisproductivity.

Venezuela Information Technology Report Q1 2009. 2009.
Venezuela Information Technology Report Q1 2009.
companiesandmarkets.com. [Online] February 12, 2009. [Cited:
April 4, 2009.] http://www.companiesandmarkets.com/Summary-
Market-Report/Venezuela-Information-Technology-Report-Q1-
2009-66481.asp.

VersionTracker. 2008. Opera 9.2. *VersionTarcker.* [Online] CBS
Interactive, 2008. [Cited: March 22, 2009.]
http://www.versiontracker.com/dyn/moreinfo/macosx/11156&vid=
400657.

VietNamNet.vn. 2009. Vietnam to widely use open source
software. *VietNamNet.vn.* [Online] VietNamNet.vn, January 6,
2009. [Cited: March 28, 2009.]
http://english.vietnamnet.vn/tech/2009/01/822425/.

W3Counter. 2009. Global Web Stats. *W3Counter.* [Online] Awio
Web Services LLC, February 1, 2009. [Cited: February 2, 2009.]
http://www.w3counter.com/globalstats.php.

Weir, Rob. 2007. A File Format Timeline. *An Antic Disposition.*
[Online] Rob Weir, June 24, 2007. [Cited: February 18, 2009.]
http://www.robweir.com/blog/2007/06/file-format-timeline.html.

Williams, Sam. 2002. Free as in Freedom. *oreilly.com.* [Online]
March 2002. [Cited: March 4, 2009.]
http://oreilly.com/openbook/freedom. 0-596-00287-4.

Wolfe, Alexander. 2007. 7 Reasons Why Linux Won't Succeed
On The Desktop. *InformationWeek .* [Online] September 19,
2007. [Cited: April 30, 2009.]
http://www.informationweek.com/shared/printableArticle.jhtml;jse
ssionid=XYI4FYT4M5PX0QSNDLPSKH0CJUNN2JVN?articleID
=201807072&_requestid=6055958.

ZDNet Research . 2007. 80% of business PCs do not support
premium Vista installs. *IT Facts.* [Online] CBS Interactive Inc.,
April 8, 2007. [Cited: March 29, 2009.]
http://blogs.zdnet.com/ITFacts/?p=12621.

Zikmund, William G. 2003. *Business Research Methods,7Th Edition.* s.l. : Thomson South-Western, 2003. 0-03-035084-0.

APPENDICES

A. The Free Software Definition

Source: http://www.fsf.org/licensing/essays/free-sw.html,

Retrieved February 21, 2009

revision 1.77, Fri Dec 19 15:25:03 2008 UTC

We maintain this free software definition to show clearly what must be true about a particular software program for it to be considered free software. From time to time we revise this definition to clarify it. If you would like to review the changes we've made, please see the History section below for more information.

Free software is a matter of liberty, not price. To understand the concept, you should think of free as in free speech, not as in free beer.

Free software is a matter of the users' freedom to run, copy, distribute, study, change and improve the software. More precisely, it refers to four kinds of freedom, for the users of the software:

- The freedom to run the program, for any purpose (freedom 0).
- The freedom to study how the program works, and adapt it to your needs (freedom 1). Access to the source code is a precondition for this.
- The freedom to redistribute copies so you can help your neighbor (freedom 2).
- The freedom to improve the program, and release your improvements (and modified versions in general) to the public, so that the whole community benefits (freedom 3). Access to the source code is a precondition for this.

A program is free software if users have all of these freedoms. Thus, you should be free to redistribute copies, either with or without modifications, either gratis or charging a fee for distribution, to anyone anywhere. Being free to do these things means (among other things) that you do not have to ask or pay for permission.

You should also have the freedom to make modifications and use them privately in your own work or play, without even mentioning that they exist. If you do publish your changes, you should not be required to notify anyone in particular, or in any particular way.

The freedom to run the program means the freedom for any kind of person or organization to use it on any kind of computer system, for any kind of overall job and purpose, without being required to communicate about it with the developer or any other specific entity. In this freedom, it is the *user's* purpose that matters, not the *developer's* purpose; you as a user are free to run a program for your purposes, and if you distribute it to someone else, she is then free to run it for her purposes, but you are not entitled to impose your purposes on her.

The freedom to redistribute copies must include binary or executable forms of the program, as well as source code, for both modified and unmodified versions. (Distributing programs in runnable form is necessary for conveniently installable free operating systems.) It is ok if there is no way to produce a binary or executable form for a certain program (since some languages don't support that feature), but you must have the freedom to redistribute such forms should you find or develop a way to make them.

In order for the freedoms to make changes, and to publish improved versions, to be meaningful, you must have access to the source code of the program. Therefore, accessibility of source code is a necessary condition for free software.

One important way to modify a program is by merging in available free subroutines and modules. If the program's license says that you cannot merge in a suitably-licensed existing module, such as if it requires you to be the copyright holder of any code you add, then the license is too restrictive to qualify as free.

In order for these freedoms to be real, they must be irrevocable as long as you do nothing wrong; if the developer of the software has the power to revoke the license, or retroactively change its terms, without your doing anything wrong to give cause, the software is not free.

However, certain kinds of rules about the manner of distributing free software are acceptable, when they don't conflict with the central freedoms. For example, copyleft (very simply stated) is the rule that when redistributing the program, you cannot add restrictions to deny other people the central freedoms. This rule does not conflict with the central freedoms; rather it protects them.

Free software does not mean non-commercial. A free program must be available for commercial use, commercial development, and commercial distribution. Commercial development of free software is no longer unusual; such free commercial software is very important. You may have paid money to get copies of free software, or you may have obtained copies at no charge. But regardless of how you got your copies, you always have the freedom to copy and change the software, even to sell copies.

Whether a change constitutes an improvement is a subjective matter. If your modifications are limited, in substance, to changes that someone else considers an improvement, that is not freedom.

However, rules about how to package a modified version are acceptable, if they don't substantively limit your freedom to release modified versions, or your freedom to make and use modified versions privately. Rules that if you make your version available in this way, you must make it available in that way also can be acceptable too, on the same condition. (Note that such a rule still leaves you the choice of whether to publish your version at all.) Rules that require release of source code to the users for versions that you put into public use are also acceptable. It is also acceptable for the license to require that, if you have distributed a modified version and a previous developer asks for a copy of it, you must send one, or that you identify yourself on your modifications.

In the GNU project, we use copyleft to protect these freedoms legally for everyone. But non-copylefted free software also exists. We believe there are important reasons why it is better to use copyleft, but if your program is non-copylefted free software, it is still basically ethical.

See Categories of Free Software for a description of how free software, copylefted software and other categories of software relate to each other.

Sometimes government export control regulations and trade sanctions can constrain your freedom to distribute copies of programs internationally. Software developers do not have the power to eliminate or override these restrictions, but what they can and must do is refuse to impose them as conditions of use of the program. In this way, the restrictions will not affect activities and people outside the jurisdictions of these governments. Thus, free software licenses must not require obedience to any export regulations as a condition of any of the essential freedoms.

Most free software licenses are based on copyright, and there are limits on what kinds of requirements can be imposed through copyright. If a copyright-based license respects freedom in the ways described above, it is unlikely to have some other sort of problem that we never anticipated (though this does happen occasionally). However, some free software licenses are based on contracts, and contracts can impose a much larger range of possible restrictions. That means there are many possible ways such a license could be unacceptably restrictive and non-free.

We can't possibly list all the ways that might happen. If a contract-based license restricts the user in an unusual way that copyright-based licenses cannot, and which isn't mentioned here as legitimate, we will have to think about it, and we will probably conclude it is non-free.

When talking about free software, it is best to avoid using terms like give away or for free, because those terms imply that the issue is about price, not freedom. Some common terms such as piracy embody opinions we hope you won't endorse. See Confusing Words and Phrases that are Worth Avoiding for a discussion of these terms. We also have a list of translations of free software into various languages.

Finally, note that criteria such as those stated in this free software definition require careful thought for their interpretation. To decide whether a specific software license qualifies as a free software license, we judge it based on these criteria to determine whether it fits their spirit as well as the precise words. If a license includes unconscionable restrictions, we reject it, even if we did not anticipate the issue in these criteria. Sometimes a license requirement raises an issue that calls for extensive thought, including discussions with a lawyer, before we can decide if the requirement is acceptable. When we reach a conclusion about a new issue, we often update these criteria to make it easier to see why certain licenses do or don't qualify.

If you are interested in whether a specific license qualifies as a free software license, see our list of licenses. If the license you are concerned with is not listed there, you can ask us about it by sending us email at <licensing@gnu.org>.

If you are contemplating writing a new license, please contact the FSF by writing to that address. The proliferation of different free software licenses means increased work for users in understanding the licenses; we may be able to help you find an existing Free Software license that meets your needs.

If that isn't possible, if you really need a new license, with our help you can ensure that the license really is a Free Software license and avoid various practical problems.

Beyond Software

, for the same reasons that software must be free, and because the manuals are in effect part of the software.

The same arguments also make sense for other kinds of works of practical use — that is to say, works that embody useful knowledge, such as educational works and reference works. Wikipedia is the best known example.

Any kind of work *can* be free, and the definition of free software has been extended to a definition of free cultural works applicable to any kind of works.

Open Source?

Another group has started using the term open source to mean something close (but not identical) to free software. We prefer the term free software because, once you have heard that it refers to freedom rather than price, it calls to mind freedom. The word open never refers to freedom.

B. The Open Source Definition (Annotated)

Source: http://www.opensource.org/docs/definition.php,

Retrieved February 21, 2009

Mon, 2006-07-24 19:04 — Ken Coar

Version 1.9

The indented, italicized sections below appear as annotations to the Open Source Definition (OSD) and are not a part of the OSD. A plain version of the OSD without annotations can be found here.

Introduction

Open source doesn't just mean access to the source code. The distribution terms of open-source software must comply with the following criteria:

1. Free Redistribution

The license shall not restrict any party from selling or giving away the software as a component of an aggregate software distribution containing programs from several different sources. The license shall not require a royalty or other fee for such sale.

> **Rationale:** By constraining the license to require free redistribution, we eliminate the temptation to throw away many long-term gains in order to make a few short-term sales dollars. If we didn't do this, there would be lots of pressure for cooperators to defect.

2. Source Code

The program must include source code, and must allow distribution in source code as well as compiled form. Where some form of a product is not distributed with source code, there must be a well-publicized means of obtaining the source code for no more than a reasonable reproduction cost preferably, downloading via the Internet without charge. The source code must be the preferred form in which a programmer would modify the program. Deliberately obfuscated source code is not allowed. Intermediate forms such as the output of a preprocessor or translator are not allowed.

> **Rationale:** We require access to un-obfuscated source code because you can't evolve programs without modifying them. Since our purpose is to make evolution easy, we require that modification be made easy.

3. Derived Works

The license must allow modifications and derived works, and must allow them to be distributed under the same terms as the license of the original software.

> **Rationale:** The mere ability to read source isn't enough to support independent peer review and rapid evolutionary selection. For rapid evolution to happen, people need to be able to experiment with and redistribute modifications.

4. Integrity of The Author's Source Code

The license may restrict source-code from being distributed in modified form *only* if the license allows the distribution of "patch files" with the source code for the purpose of modifying the program at build time. The license must explicitly permit distribution of software built from modified source code. The license may require derived works to carry a different name or version number from the original software

> **Rationale:** Encouraging lots of improvement is a good thing, but users have a right to know who is responsible for the software they are using. Authors and maintainers have reciprocal right to know what they're being asked to

support and protect their reputations.

Accordingly, an open-source license must guarantee that source be readily available, but may require that it be distributed as pristine base sources plus patches. In this way, "unofficial" changes can be made available but readily distinguished from the base source.

5. No Discrimination Against Persons or Groups

The license must not discriminate against any person or group of persons.

Rationale: In order to get the maximum benefit from the process, the maximum diversity of persons and groups should be equally eligible to contribute to open sources. Therefore we forbid any open-source license from locking anybody out of the process.

Some countries, including the United States, have export restrictions for certain types of software. An OSD-conformant license may warn licensees of applicable restrictions and remind them that they are obliged to obey the law; however, it may not incorporate such restrictions itself.

6. No Discrimination Against Fields of Endeavor

The license must not restrict anyone from making use of the program in a specific field of endeavor. For example, it may not restrict the program from being used in a business, or from being used for genetic research.

Rationale: The major intention of this clause is to prohibit license traps that prevent open source from being used commercially. We want commercial users to join our community, not feel excluded from it.

7. Distribution of License

The rights attached to the program must apply to all to whom the program is redistributed without the need for execution of an additional license by those parties.

> **Rationale:** This clause is intended to forbid closing up software by indirect means such as requiring a non-disclosure agreement.

8. License Must Not Be Specific to a Product

The rights attached to the program must not depend on the program's being part of a particular software distribution. If the program is extracted from that distribution and used or distributed within the terms of the program's license, all parties to whom the program is redistributed should have the same rights as those that are granted in conjunction with the original software distribution.

> **Rationale:** This clause forecloses yet another class of license traps.

9. License Must Not Restrict Other Software

The license must not place restrictions on other software that is distributed along with the licensed software. For example, the license must not insist that all other programs distributed on the same medium must be open-source software.

> **Rationale:** Distributors of open-source software have the right to make their own choices about their own software.
>
> Yes, the GPL is conformant with this requirement. Software linked with GPLed libraries only inherits the GPL if it forms a single work, not any software with which they are merely distributed.

10. License Must Be Technology-Neutral

No provision of the license may be predicated on any individual technology or style of interface.

Rationale: This provision is aimed specifically at licenses which require an explicit gesture of assent in order to establish a contract between licensor and licensee. Provisions mandating so-called "click-wrap" may conflict with important methods of software distribution such as FTP download, CD-ROM anthologies, and web mirroring; such provisions may also hinder code re-use. Conformant licenses must allow for the possibility that **(a)** redistribution of the software will take place over non-Web channels that do not support click-wrapping of the download, and that **(b)** the covered code (or re-used portions of covered code) may run in a non-GUI environment that cannot support popup dialogues.

C. Survey Questionnaires

Preliminary survey of most commonly used work-related applications

القطاع/Sector: □الخاص/Private □العام/Public	الجنس/Gender: □أنثى/Female □ذكر/Male	العمر/Age: _____
مجال الوظيفة / Job Category (إدارة،تسويق،محاسبة،تقني،إلخ): _____	مجال العمل/Industry (حكومي،عقار،اتصالات،إلخ): _____

Please answer all the following questions, but in one language only	برجاء الإجابة على جميع الأسئلة التالية، ولكن بلغة واحدة فقط
1. Describe your experience using computers at work. □ **Very easy** to use computers □ **Easy** to use computers □ **Somewhat difficult** to use computers □ **Hard** to use computers □ **Very hard** to use computers	1. كيف تجد تجربتك مع الحاسب الآلي أثناء العمل ؟ □ **سهل جداً** أن أستخدم الحاسب □ **سهل** أن أستخدم الحاسب □ **أعاني بعض الصعوبات** أثناء استخدام الحاسب □ **صعب** أن أستخدم الحاسب □ **صعب جداً** أن أستخدم الحاسب
2. How much do you depend on printing at work ? □ I never print □ I rarely print □ I very frequently print	2. ما مدى اعتمادك على الطباعة من البرامج أثناء العمل في المكتب؟ □ لا أطبع أبداً □ أطبع نادراً □ أطبع كثيراً
3. How often do you use e-mail at work ? □ Never □ Rarely □ Very frequently	3. كم تستخدم بريد العمل الإلكتروني أثناء عملك ؟ □ أبداً □ نادراً □ كثيراً
4. How often do you read or create work-related information in the Arabic language ? □ Never □ Rarely □ Very frequently	4. إلى أي مدى تحتاج لقراءة أو كتابة معلومات العمل الإلكترونية باللغة العربية ؟ □ أبداً □ نادراً □ كثيراً
5. How often do you deal with PDF (Acrobat) files at work ? □ Never □ Rarely □ Very frequently	5. ما مدى استخدامك لملفات أكروبات (PDF) أثناء عملك ؟ □ أبداً □ نادراً □ كثيراً
6. Do you access files centralized on a network server at work ? □ Yes □ No □ I don't know	6. هل تحتاج لفتح ملفات على جهاز مركزي (سيرفر) بشبكة العمل ؟ □ نعم □ لا □ لا أعلم
7. How often does your work require access to information through your organization's intranet or web applications ? □ Never □ Rarely □ Very frequently □ I don't know	7. إلى أي مدى يحتاج عملك لتصفح معلومات العمل على شبكة (انترانت) العمل أو برامج العمل المبنية على متصفح الويب ؟ □ أبداً □ نادراً □ كثيراً □ لا أعلم
8. What are the **ten most-used** work-related applications and functions you use your work computer for (you can use some of your previous answers here if they are valid) ? _____ _____ _____ _____ _____ _____ _____	8. ما هي **أكثر عشرة** برامج ومهام متعلقة بالعمل تستخدم لأجلها الحاسب الآلي في العمل (يمكن ذكر بعض ما سبق من إجابتك إن كان من ضمنها) ؟

Post-experiment survey of subject profile and perception evaluation

Field	Subject 1	Subject 2	Subject 3	Subject 4	Subject 5
Serial Number	1	2	3	4	5
Name					
Gender (M/F)	f	m	m	m	m
Age	40	16	20	45	34
0-Public/1-Private Sector			1	0	1
Industry			Education	Education	Education
Specialization			Admin	Academic	Academic
Technical Proficiency (0-3)	1	3	1	2	2
Ease of Vista (0-3)	3	3	1	2	2
Ease of Linux (0-3)	2	2	2	1	1
Satisfaction with Vista (0-3)	3	2	0	2	2
Satisfaction with Linux (0-3)	0y	2y	2n	2y	2y
Agree to use Vista at work (Y/N)	y	y	y	y	y
Agree to use Linux at work (Y/N)	v	v	—	v	v
Preferred solution at work (L/V)	quicker	I can work	Nothing	accustomed to it	accustomed to it
Liked of the Vista solution	Nothing	the delayed response	Not practical	Nothing	response, adaptability, different UI
Disliked of the Vista solution	quickly adapted, close to Vista,	nice interface, easy to learn	Overall good	No problems	speed
Liked of the Linux solution	not accustomed to	Nothing	To many menu options	Nothing	Nothing
Disliked of the Linux solution					

D. Detailed Installation and Configuration of OSS Solution

As per the results of phase 1 and 2 findings (discussed in chapters 4 and 5 of this study), the Ubuntu Linux distribution has proven user-friendly, most popular, and highly supportable in an organizational environment. As such, it was chosen as the Operating System to base the OSS comparison solution upon.

Ubuntu version 9.04 was installed on the first VirtualBox virtual machine using Ubuntu's guided setup default options. Other applications found to be required through the results of the previous phases; 1 and 2 are: the PDF viewer (Document Viewer 2.26.1), the web browser (Firefox version 3.0.9), the word processor, presentation, and spreadsheet applications (OpenOffice.org version 3.0.1), the e-mail and calendaring/scheduling application (Evolution version 2.26.1). All part of the Ubuntu distribution and required no further installation steps.

As organizational desktop computers are usually delivered pre-configured to employees, configuration took place on the Ubuntu desktop solution in order to deliver an easier experience to first-time Windows users as they are migrated to Ubuntu Linux. Changes from the default settings took place in the following aspects, and as many may not be familiar with how these changes are done in Ubuntu Linux, screen captures are included in place of lengthy procedure explanations:

- Installed the VirtualBox Linux Additions in order to enable features such as "Shared Folders".

- Created a start.sh file which includes the following command line to map the shared folder: sudo mount.vboxsf New /home/test/Desktop/Start. This is in order to map the shared folder "New" to the mount point "/home/test/Desktop/Start". The Intaj productivity benchmark will be run from this shared folder.
- The dual taskbar layout was changed to a single taskbar layout as Windows users were more accustomed to the later.

Figure 25: Ubuntu Dual Taskbar Layout

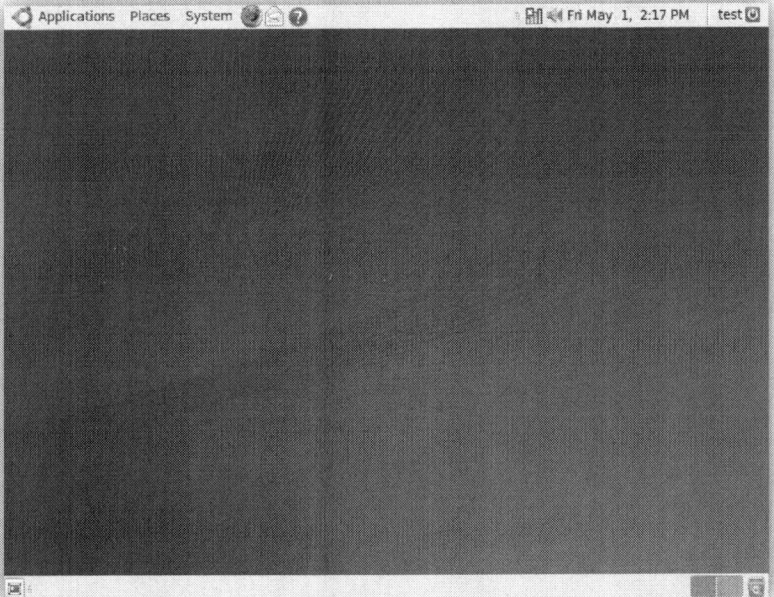

Figure 26: Ubuntu Single Taskbar Layout

- Taskbar main menu was edited in order to simplify the number of available applications to the user.

Figure 27: Editing the Ubuntu Main Menu

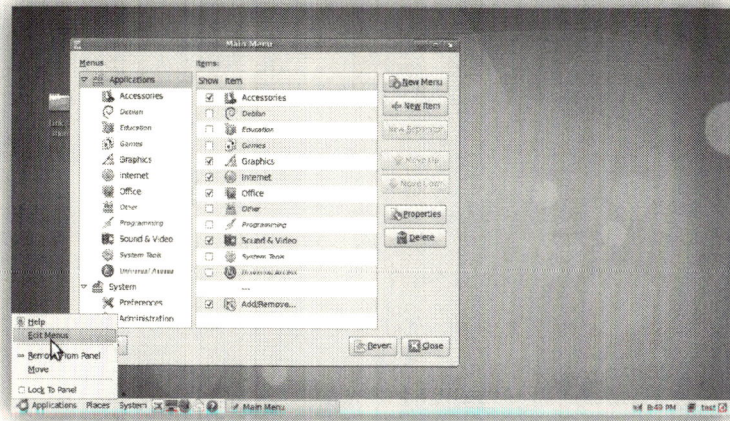

- Changed the File Management default view to "List View".

Figure 28: Changing Ubuntu File Management Preferences

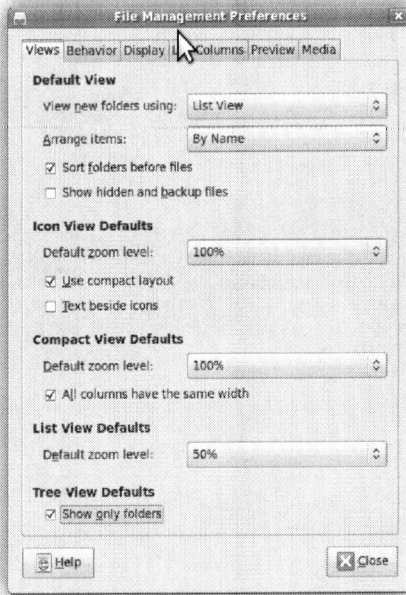

- Configured the keyboard's Windows Key to start the taskbar's main menu.

Figure 29: Mapping Window Key to Main Menu

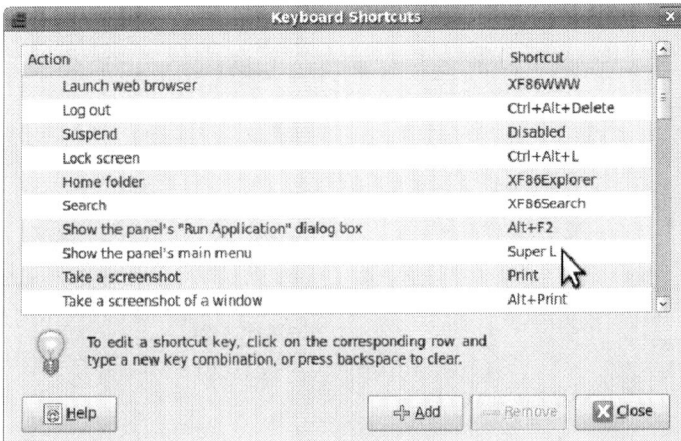

- Mouse pointer size was increased.

Figure 30: Increasing Pointer Size

- Installed Arabic language related additions except for translations.

Figure 31: Adding Arabic Capability

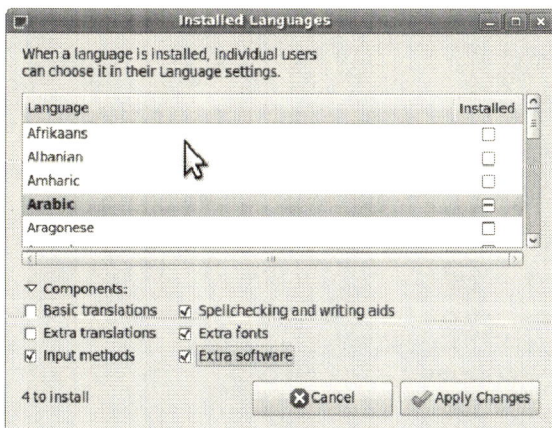

- Added the Arabic (Bahrain) keyboard layout.

Figure 32: Adding Arabic Keyboard

- Configured the keyboard layout switching controls.

Figure 33: Configuring Keyboard Layout Switching

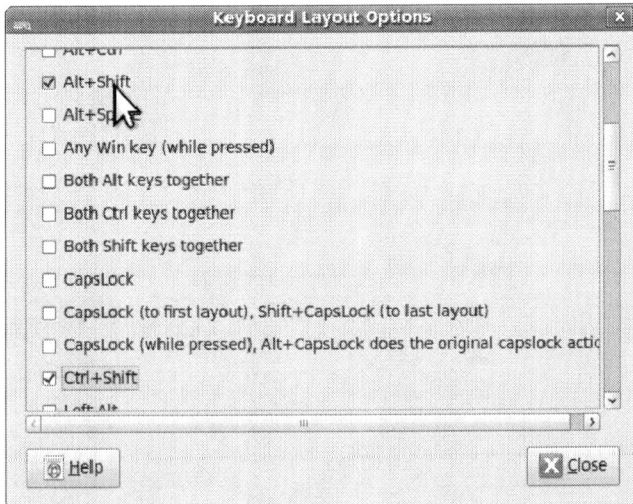

- Added the "Keyboard Indicator" panel to the taskbar.

Figure 34: Adding Keyboard Indicator

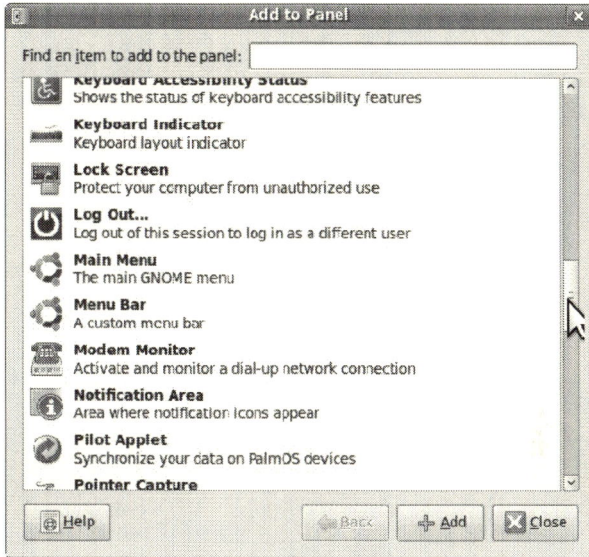

- Installed extra free fonts through the "Ubuntu restricted extras" package.

Figure 35: Installing Extra Fonts

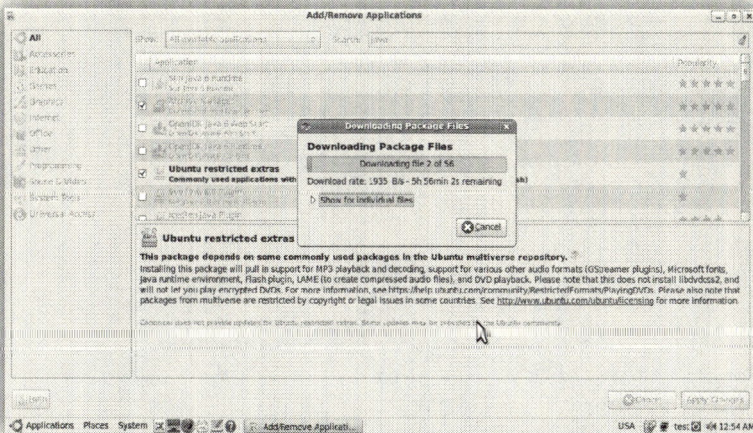

177

- All the latest Ubuntu software updates and patches were applied automatically.

Figure 36: Updating Ubuntu

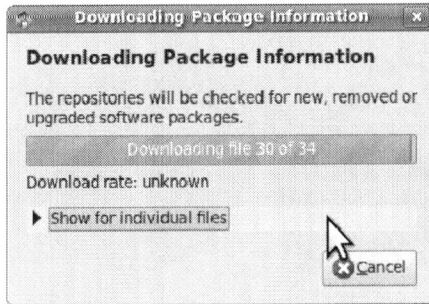

- Installed Sun Java Runtime Environment 6.0 and Browser Plug-in.
- Installed Adobe Flash 10 Browser Plug-in.

Figure 37: Installing Adobe Flash Plug-in

- Configured OpenOffice.org options to enable support for Complex Text Layout (CTL). Necessary for Arabic text input.

Figure 38: Enabling Arabic in OpenOffice.org

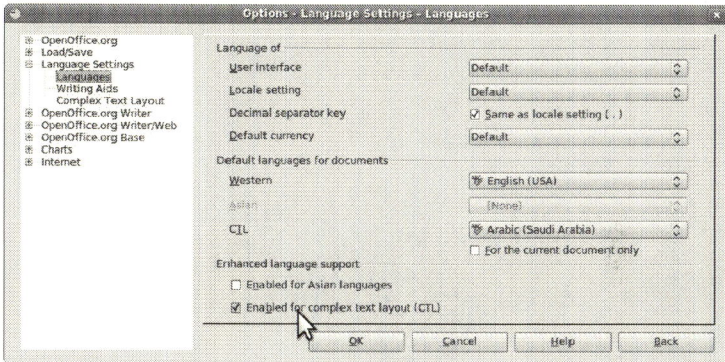

- Configured all CTL basic fonts in OpenOffice.org to AlMohanad 14pt except "Heading" which was configured at 16pt.

Figure 39: Configured OpenOffice.org Default Arabic Fonts

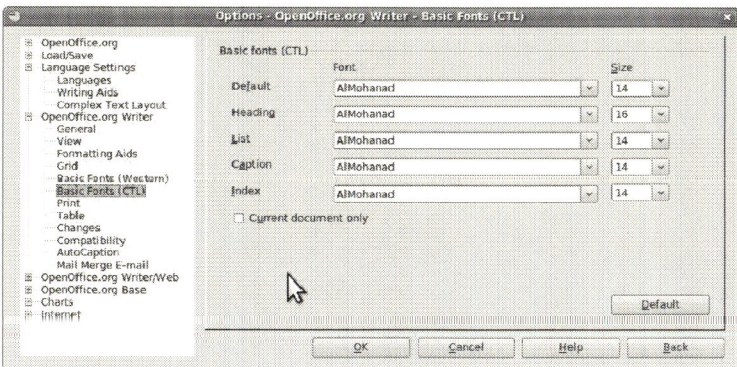

- The Evolution e-mail client was setup with the following server settings in order to be able to send and receive e-mail:

  Username: the_test@live.com

  Password: desktop

  Incoming server: pop3.live.com

  Use secure connection: SSL

  Authentication type: password

  Outgoing server: smtp.live.com

  Use Secure Connection: TLS Encryption

  Authentication Type: Login

- Upgraded to OpenOffice.org 3.1 by adding the following sources to *Software Sources*, *Third Party Software* tab: "deb http://ppa.launchpad.net/openoffice-pkgs/ppa/ubuntu jaunty main" and "deb-src http://ppa.launchpad.net/openoffice-pkgs/ppa/ubuntu jaunty main". The following code was then copied to an empty file and in *Software Sources*, under Authentication tab, the "Import Key File" button was used to import the file. The old OpenOffice.org was removed by updating the system then running "*sudo apt-get remove language-support-en language-support-translations-en openoffice.org-help-en-gb openoffice.org-l10n-en-gb openoffice.org-l10n-en-za thunderbird-locale-en-gb*". The new OpenOffice.org was then installed from *"Add/Remove..."*.

-----BEGIN PGP PUBLIC KEY BLOCK-----

Version: SKS 1.0.10

mI0ESXanRwEEAOTPu1sTcJChTjkA9LkIh6WqiBgPzxN
Y2p8w18Qt/cE3ev4VyjiIadZtr+fh
C+kuRRQuRinLV+MzeD7Od3uqyR1plc90IqUeLeKJMgXf
CoGMmKwng0qD2gpevIvEEpdImsRo
1hutsyRxAL3o/NfFpovg6dWC27Y1Vwwma8UIL5wXABE
BAAG0K0xhdW5jaHBhZCBQQUEEgZm9y
IE9wZW5PZmZpY2Uub3JnIFNjcmliYmxlcnOltgQTAQIAI
AUCSXanRwIbAwYLCQgHAwIEFQII
AwQWAgMBAh4BAheAAAoJEGDREhckfRz/4QoEAOJ4
29PsO5oi1xsnX/IraHACYpHNvk4KVghu
cY2p6J8M0WTTlfls96jRYGIDBDuyZcfW0W+VJIaiu28u2
Y9zEnXTWHMIIk6PiOmLPxXofgDf
IKRqvBFYdRD8+33TBeD6u6qajNOLYTL08dnqCfVqmJT
GZxqXTmYIOF1NdIs0KIF/
=1y5I

-----END PGP PUBLIC KEY BLOCK-----

- Installed the Mint Menu through Synaptics after adding "deb http://packages.linuxmint.com gloria main" to the sources. This menu replaced the default Gnome menu on the panel (taskbar).

- Installed wallpaper and the Mac OS X theme from http://gnome-look.org

E. Sample Tabulated Experiment Data

	Vtask1	Vtask2	Vtask3	Vtask4	Vtask5	Vtask6	Vtask7	Vtask8	Vtotal	Ltask1	Ltask2	Ltask3	Ltask4	Ltask5	Ltask6	Ltask7	Ltask8	Ltotal	G an / Ag e	
1	0:00:16	0:00:24	0:00:22	0:00:34	0:00:16	0:00:21	0:00:52	0:00:44	0:03:36	0:00:10	0:00:24	0:00:17	0:01:10	0:00:33	0:00:11	0:00:33	0:02:06	0:08:15	m	16
2	0:00:10	0:00:21	0:00:22	0:00:34	0:00:27	0:00:11	0:00:26	0:01:02	0:03:13	0:00:16	0:01:03	0:01:42	0:01:10	0:00:28	0:00:54	0:00:33	0:02:06	0:02:42	m	20
3	0:01:05	0:00:08	0:03:13	0:00:34	0:00:44	0:01:07	0:00:41	0:01:02	0:08:50	0:00:16	0:01:03	0:01:42	0:01:10	0:00:28	0:01:58	0:02:58	0:04:05	0:08:08	m	46
4	0:00:44	0:00:17	0:00:22	0:00:10	0:00:27	0:00:11	0:00:26	0:00:44	0:02:58	0:00:16	0:00:24	0:01:42	0:01:10	0:00:15	0:00:22	0:00:25	0:00:34	0:02:51	f	34
5	0:00:44	0:00:24	0:00:18	0:00:34	0:00:44	0:00:21	0:00:52	0:01:02	0:03:26	0:00:16	0:00:24	0:00:28	0:00:22	0:00:15	0:00:33	0:00:25	0:00:39	0:03:14	m	39
6	0:00:07	0:00:06	0:01:44	0:00:42	0:00:15	0:00:27	0:00:27	0:00:43	0:03:36	0:00:11	0:00:05	0:00:48	0:00:07	0:00:14	0:00:06	0:00:20	0:00:34	0:03:14	f	14
7	0:00:07	0:00:07	0:01:45	0:00:11	0:00:18	0:00:07	0:00:31	0:00:32	0:03:29	0:00:04	0:00:09	0:00:19	0:00:07	0:00:13	0:00:10	0:00:16	0:01:20	0:02:28	m	39
8	0:00:23	0:02:25	0:01:56	0:00:22	0:00:15	0:00:45	0:00:54	0:02:42	0:05:04	0:00:12	0:00:07	0:00:48	0:02:17	0:02:44	0:01:58	0:02:58	0:04:05	0:04:18	m	24
9	0:00:52	0:00:37	0:00:29	0:00:11	0:01:19	0:00:05	0:01:20	0:00:28	0:04:51	0:00:12	0:01:09	0:01:45	0:00:21	0:00:14	0:00:06	0:00:26	0:00:39	0:04:49	m	43
10	0:00:42	0:00:17	0:01:56	0:03:16	0:02:34	0:00:25	0:00:13	0:01:08	0:07:06	0:00:25	0:00:18	0:01:00	0:00:45	0:00:39	0:00:27	0:00:39	0:00:31	0:17:30	f	46
11	0:00:29	0:00:37	0:00:31	0:01:03	0:00:18	0:00:10	0:00:13	0:00:38	0:03:51	0:00:47	0:00:05	0:01:43	0:00:12	0:00:11	0:00:20	0:00:25	0:00:31	0:04:18	m	20
12	0:00:16	0:00:18	0:01:09	0:00:21	0:00:24	0:00:28	0:00:35	0:00:50	0:04:25	0:00:07	0:00:04	0:00:28	0:00:20	0:00:08	0:00:10	0:00:16	0:00:35	0:09:08	f	41
13	0:00:56	0:01:06	0:02:02	0:01:07	0:00:29	0:01:12	0:00:55	0:01:23	0:09:12	0:00:25	0:00:16	0:01:04	0:01:52	0:01:23	0:00:26	0:01:14	0:01:25	0:05:19	f	28
14	0:00:36	0:00:18	0:00:36	0:00:26	0:00:37	0:00:15	0:00:46	0:00:38	0:04:36	0:00:39	0:01:02	0:00:28	0:00:48	0:00:38	0:00:23	0:00:35	0:00:41	0:04:22	f	27
15	0:00:11	0:00:11	0:00:25	0:00:16	0:00:22	0:00:28	0:00:28	0:00:58	0:03:22	0:00:17	0:00:35	0:00:29	0:00:22	0:00:23	0:01:07	0:00:25	0:00:41	0:04:22	f	27

Sheet1 / Sheet2 / Sheet3

F. Source Code for "Intaj" (A Productivity Benchmark in Java)

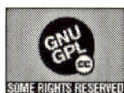

```
/*
Name      : Intaj 1.0
Author    : Abubakr Bassam Bokhowa
Design    : Bassam Bokhowa
Date      : May 14, 2009
About     : Productivity Benchmark Using Java
*/


import java.awt.Font;
import java.awt.GraphicsEnvironment;
import java.io.PrintStream;
import javax.swing.JFrame;
import javax.swing.JScrollPane;
import javax.swing.JTextPane;
import javax.swing.SwingUtilities;
import javax.swing.UIManager;
import javax.swing.event.CaretEvent;
import javax.swing.event.CaretListener;
import javax.swing.text.AbstractDocument;
import javax.swing.text.BadLocationException;
import javax.swing.text.Document;
import javax.swing.text.JTextComponent;
import javax.swing.text.View;
import java.awt.*;
import java.awt.event.*;
import javax.swing.*;
import java.text.*;
import java.util.*;
import java.io.*;

public class ProdBench extends JPanel implements ActionListener{

        static protected JTextArea taskText;
        static protected JScrollPane scrollbars;
        protected JButton cmdDone, cmdStart, cmdLngSwitch;
        static ElapsedTime Tasktmr = new ElapsedTime();
        static int taskcount, lasttask, currenttask;
        static long totaltime;
        static String[] tasks;
        static String logfile, LangState;
        Font cmdFont, txtFont;
        boolean OSwindows;
```

```java
        String OS;

        public ProdBench(){

//set the container's background color & layout
            setBackground(new Color(185,185,200));
            setLayout(null);
            //OS=System.getProperty("os.name");
            //OS=OS.substring(0,7);
            //OS="WINDOWS";
            GraphicsEnvironment.getLocalGraphicsEnvironment().getAllFonts();
            File f= new File("C:/Windows");
            if (f.isDirectory()){
                    OSwindows=true;
                    cmdFont = new Font("Dialog.plain", Font.PLAIN, 12);
                    txtFont = new Font("Dialog.plain", Font.PLAIN, 14);
            }
            else{
                    OSwindows=false;
                    cmdFont = new Font("Dialog.plain",Font.PLAIN, 8);
                    txtFont = new Font("Traditional Arabic",Font.PLAIN, 16);
            }

//create scrollable text area
            taskText = new JTextArea("");
            taskText.setEnabled(false);
            taskText.setDisabledTextColor(new Color(0,0,0));
            taskText.setLineWrap(true);
            taskText.setSize(170,77);
            taskText.setMargin(new Insets(0,3,0,3));
            final AbstractDocument doc = (AbstractDocument)
taskText.getDocument();
            doc.putProperty("i18n", Boolean.TRUE);
//Change text font size and style(BOLD or ITALIC or PLAIN) here
            //taskText.setFont(new
Font(taskText.getFont().getFontName(),Font.BOLD,14));
            taskText.setFont(txtFont);

        taskText.setComponentOrientation(ComponentOrientation.RIGHT_TO_LEFT);
            scrollbars = new JScrollPane(taskText);
            scrollbars.setSize(170,77);
            scrollbars.setLocation(2,1);

//create and setup buttons
            cmdDone = new
JButton("\u0627\u0646\u062a\u0647\u064a\u062a");
            cmdDone.setEnabled(false);
            cmdDone.setSize(65,18);
            cmdDone.setLocation(25,80);
            cmdDone.setFont(cmdFont);//change button font size here
            cmdDone.setActionCommand("done");
            cmdStart = new JButton("\u0627\u0628\u062f\u0623");
            cmdStart.setSize(65,18);
            cmdStart.setLocation(90,80);
            cmdStart.setFont(cmdFont);//change button font size here
            cmdStart.setActionCommand("start");
            cmdLngSwitch = new JButton("En");
            cmdLngSwitch.setSize(19,18);
```

```java
                cmdLngSwitch.setMargin(new Insets(0,0,0,0));
                cmdLngSwitch.setLocation(1,80);

        cmdLngSwitch.setFont(cmdLngSwitch.getFont().deriveFont((float)10));//change
button font size here
                cmdLngSwitch.setActionCommand("switch");
                LangState="Ar";


//listen for actions on buttons
                cmdDone.addActionListener(this);
                cmdStart.addActionListener(this);
                cmdLngSwitch.addActionListener(this);

            `   add(scrollbars);
                add(cmdDone);
                add(cmdStart);
                add(cmdLngSwitch);
        }
//procedure to reset the scrollbars
        protected static void resetScrollBar(){
                SwingUtilities.invokeLater(new Runnable(){
                        public void run(){
                                scrollbars.getVerticalScrollBar().setValue(0);
                        }
                });
        }

        public void actionPerformed(ActionEvent e) {
                if ("start".equals(e.getActionCommand())) {//what happens when user
presses start button
                        if (currenttask==0){
                                lasttask=currenttask;
                                currenttask=currenttask+1;
                                taskText.setText("");
                                taskText.setText(tasks[currenttask]);
                                resetScrollBar();
                        }
                        else{
                                cmdStart.setEnabled(false);
                                cmdDone.setEnabled(true);
                                Tasktmr.StartCounter();
                        }
                } else if ("done".equals(e.getActionCommand())) {//what happens
when user presses done button
                        String elapsedtime;
                        cmdDone.setEnabled(false);
                        cmdStart.setEnabled(true);
                        elapsedtime = Tasktmr.ElapsedTime();
                        totaltime=totaltime+Tasktmr.elapsed;

//set the values for lasttask, currenttask etc.
                        if (currenttask==taskcount){
                                lasttask=currenttask;
                                currenttask=0;
                                taskText.setText("");
                                taskText.setText(tasks[currenttask]);
                                resetScrollBar();
```

```
                                }
                                else{
                                        lasttask=currenttask;
                                        currenttask=currenttask+1;
                                        taskText.setText("");
                                        taskText.setText(tasks[currenttask]);
                                        resetScrollBar();
                                }

//write to log(task, time)
                                if (currenttask==1){
                                }
                                else{
                                        try{
                                                FileWriter fstream = new
FileWriter(logfile,true);
                                                BufferedWriter out = new
BufferedWriter(fstream);
                                                out.write(lasttask + "," +
Tasktmr.StartedTime() + "," + Tasktmr.CurrentTime() + "," + elapsedtime);
                                                out.newLine();
//close the output stream
                                                out.close();
                                        }catch (Exception e1){//catch exception if any
                                                System.err.println("Error: " +
e1.getMessage());
                                        }
                                        if (lasttask==taskcount){
                                        try{
//write stats to the logfile
                                                FileWriter fstream = new
FileWriter(logfile,true);
                                                BufferedWriter out = new
BufferedWriter(fstream);
                                                SimpleDateFormat dateFormat = new
SimpleDateFormat("HH:mm:ss");

        dateFormat.setTimeZone(TimeZone.getTimeZone("GMT"));
                                                out.write(",,Total Time:," +
dateFormat.format(new Date(totaltime)));
                                                out.close();
                                        }catch (Exception e1){
                                                System.err.println("Error: " +
e1.getMessage());
                                        }
//change the logfile name after each time all tasks are finished
                                                logfile=getDateTime()+".txt";
                                                totaltime=0;
                                        }
                                }
                        } else if ("switch".equals(e.getActionCommand())){
                                if (LangState=="Ar"){
                                        int i;
                                        try{
                                                BufferedReader in = new
BufferedReader(new InputStreamReader(new FileInputStream("entasks.txt")));
                                                for(i=0;i<=taskcount;i++)
                                                {
```

186

```java
                                                    String nxttask =
in.readLine();
                                                    tasks[i]=nxttask;
                                        }
                                        in.close();
                                }catch(Exception e3){
                                        System.out.println(e3.getMessage());
                                }
                                cmdStart.setText("Start");
                                cmdDone.setText("Done");
                                cmdStart.setLocation(25,80);
                                cmdDone.setLocation(90,80);

        cmdStart.setFont(cmdStart.getFont().deriveFont((float)11));

        cmdDone.setFont(cmdDone.getFont().deriveFont((float)11));
                                cmdLngSwitch.setText("Ar");
                                LangState="En";
                                logfile=getDateTime()+".txt";
                                totaltime=0;
                                currenttask=0;
                                taskText.setText(tasks[currenttask]);
                                resetScrollBar();
                                cmdDone.setEnabled(false);
                                cmdStart.setEnabled(true);

        taskText.setComponentOrientation(ComponentOrientation.LEFT_TO_RIGHT);
                                taskText.setFont(new
Font("Dialog.plain",Font.PLAIN,12));
                        } else{
                                int i;
                                try{
                                        BufferedReader in = new
BufferedReader(new InputStreamReader(new FileInputStream("artasks.txt"),"Unicode"));
                                        for(i=0;i<=taskcount;i++)
                                        {
                                                String nxttask =
in.readLine();
                                                tasks[i]=nxttask;
                                        }
                                        in.close();
                                }catch(Exception e3){
                                        System.out.println(e3.getMessage());
                                }
                                cmdStart.setText("\u0625\u0628\u062f\u0623");

        cmdDone.setText("\u0625\u0646\u062a\u0647\u064a\u062a");
                                cmdStart.setLocation(90,80);
                                cmdDone.setLocation(25,80);
                                cmdStart.setFont(cmdFont);
                                cmdDone.setFont(cmdFont);
                                cmdLngSwitch.setText("En");
                                LangState="Ar";
                                logfile=getDateTime()+".txt";
                                totaltime=0;
                                currenttask=0;
                                taskText.setText(tasks[currenttask]);
                                resetScrollBar();
```

```
                                cmdDone.setEnabled(false);
                                cmdStart.setEnabled(true);

        taskText.setComponentOrientation(ComponentOrientation.RIGHT_TO_LEFT);
                                taskText.setFont(txtFont);
                        }
                        }
                }

        private static void createAndShowGUI() {

//create and set up the window.
                final JFrame frame = new JFrame("Intaj");
                frame.setDefaultCloseOperation(JFrame.EXIT_ON_CLOSE);
                frame.setSize(174,100);
                frame.setLocation(75,0);
                frame.setUndecorated(true);
                frame.setAlwaysOnTop(true);
                frame.setResizable(false);

//Create and set up the content pane.
                ProdBench newContentPane = new ProdBench();
                newContentPane.setOpaque(true); //content panes must be opaque
                frame.setContentPane(newContentPane);

//the following code is to allow the dragging of the frame even
//though it's undecorated and doesn't have a titlebar
                final Point origin = new Point();
                frame.addMouseListener(new MouseAdapter() {
                public void mousePressed(MouseEvent e) {
                        origin.x = e.getX();
                        origin.y = e.getY();
                }
                });
                frame.addMouseMotionListener(new MouseMotionAdapter() {
                public void mouseDragged(MouseEvent e) {
                        Point p = frame.getLocation();
//make sure the window doesnt go outside the 0,0 bound of the screen
                        if ((((p.y + e.getY() - origin.y)<=0) && ((p.x + e.getX() -
origin.x)<=0))
                                frame.setLocation(0,0);
                        else if ((p.x + e.getX() - origin.x)<=0)
                                frame.setLocation(0, p.y + e.getY() - origin.y);
                        else if ((p.y + e.getY() - origin.y)<=0)
                                frame.setLocation(p.x + e.getX() - origin.x, 0);
                        else
                                frame.setLocation(p.x + e.getX() - origin.x, p.y +
e.getY() - origin.y);
                }
                });
//allow dragging of frame through the text box
                final Point origin2 = new Point();
                taskText.addMouseListener(new MouseAdapter() {
                public void mousePressed(MouseEvent e) {
                        origin2.x = e.getX();
                        origin2.y = e.getY();
                }
                });
```

```java
                    taskText.addMouseMotionListener(new MouseMotionAdapter() {
                    public void mouseDragged(MouseEvent e) {
                            Point p = frame.getLocation();
//make sure the window doesnt go outside the 0,0 bound of the screen
                            if (((p.y + e.getY() - origin2.y)<=0) && ((p.x + e.getX() -
origin2.x)<=0))
                                    frame.setLocation(0,0);
                    else if ((p.x + e.getX() - origin2.x)<=0)
                            frame.setLocation(0, p.y + e.getY() - origin2.y);
                    else if ((p.y + e.getY() - origin2.y)<=0)
                            frame.setLocation(p.x + e.getX() - origin2.x, 0);
                    else
                            frame.setLocation(p.x + e.getX() - origin2.x, p.y
+ e.getY() - origin2.y);
                    }
                    });

//display the window.
                    frame.setVisible(true);

//change this to total number of tasks
                    taskcount = 8;
                    tasks = new String[taskcount+1];

//read all the tasks in arabic from a text file, line by line, using unicode encoding
                    int i;
                    try{
                            BufferedReader in = new BufferedReader(new
InputStreamReader(new FileInputStream("artasks.txt"),"Unicode"));
                            for(i=0;i<=taskcount;i++)
                            {
                                    String nxttask = in.readLine();
                                    tasks[i]=nxttask;
                            }
                            in.close();
                    }catch(Exception e3){
                            System.out.println(e3.getMessage());
                    }

//set the task description text
                    currenttask=0;
                    taskText.setText(tasks[0]);

//set logfile path
                    logfile=getDateTime()+".txt";

//reset scrollbar
                    resetScrollBar();
            }

        public static void main(String[] args){
//schedule a job for the event-dispatching thread:
                    javax.swing.SwingUtilities.invokeLater(new Runnable() {
                            public void run() {
                                    createAndShowGUI();
                            }});
            }
//simple function that returns current date and time as a string
```

189

```java
        public static String getDateTime(){
                DateFormat dateFormat = new SimpleDateFormat("yyyy-MM-dd
HH.mm.ss");
                Date date = new Date();
                return dateFormat.format(date);
        }

}
//this class calculates elapsed time between calling the
//startcounter() function and the elapsedtime() function
class ElapsedTime{
        public long startTime;
        public long elapsed;
        long currentTime, currTime;
        SimpleDateFormat dateFormat;

        public void StartCounter(){
                dateFormat = new SimpleDateFormat("HH:mm:ss");
                startTime = System.currentTimeMillis();
        }

        public String ElapsedTime(){
                currentTime = System.currentTimeMillis();
                dateFormat.setTimeZone(TimeZone.getTimeZone("GMT"));
                elapsed = currentTime - startTime;
                return dateFormat.format(new Date(elapsed));
        }

//returns current time only
        public String CurrentTime(){
                currTime = System.currentTimeMillis();
                dateFormat.setTimeZone(TimeZone.getTimeZone("GMT"));
                return dateFormat.format(new Date(currTime));
        }

//returns the time at which the counter was started
        public String StartedTime(){
                dateFormat.setTimeZone(TimeZone.getTimeZone("GMT"));
                return dateFormat.format(new Date(startTime));
        }
}
```

G. Test Script Files: Arabic and English

اقرأ التعليمات الآتية وإضغط زر "ابدأ" قبل التنفيذ، وعند الانتهاء إضغط زر "انتهيت". يمكنك تحريك نافذة البرنامج.

١. اضغط "ابدأ" ثم افتح الملف Exam.doc من المجلد New الذي على سطح المكتب ...

٢. اضغط "ابدأ" ثم اطبع Exam.doc ...

٣. اضغط "ابدأ" ثم احفظ Exam.doc في المجلد Auto الذي على سطح المكتب ...

٤. اضغط "ابدأ" ثم انسخ الملف Exam.doc من المجلد Auto إلى سطح المكتب ...

٥. اضغط "ابدأ" ثم افتح الملف Exam.doc من سطح المكتب وغير حجم الخط لسطر واحد ثم انسخه (سيتم لصقه في الخطوة القادمة) ...

٦. اضغط "ابدأ" ثم افتح مستند جديد والصق الفقرة المنسوخة سابقاً فيه ...

٧. اضغط "ابدأ" ثم احفظ المستند الجديد على سطح المكتب باسمك وباستعمال حروف عربية ...

٨. اضغط "ابدأ" ثم ابعث المستند الجديد كمرفق برسالة بريد إلكتروني إلى the_test@live.com

Read the instructions and press "Start" before performing them, and "Done" once completed. This window is movable.

1. Press "Start" then open the file EXAM.DOC from the "New" desktop folder ...

2. Press "Start" then print the EXAM.DOC document ...

3. Press "Start" then save EXAM.DOC in the "Auto" desktop folder ...

4. Press "Start" then copy the EXAM.DOC file from the "Auto" folder to the desktop ...

5. Press "Start" then open the EXAM.DOC file from the desktop and enlarge the font size of one sentence then copy it (pasting is in the next step) ...

6. Press "Start" then create a new document and paste the previously copied paragraph into it ...

7. Press "Start" then save the new document to the desktop with your name using Arabic letters ...

8. Press "Start" then send the new document attached with an e-mail to: the_test@live.com

H. Research Data Figures

Historical data from SurveyWare's browser satisfaction poll

Day	Firefox	Opera	Safari	Internet Explorer
8/15/2008	50.00%	8.33%	25.00%	16.67%
8/16/2008	72.73%	13.64%	9.09%	4.55%
8/17/2008	70.00%	15.00%	15.00%	0.00%
8/18/2008	73.91%	8.70%	8.70%	8.70%
8/19/2008	60.00%	0.00%	26.67%	13.33%
8/20/2008	50.00%	1.92%	44.23%	3.85%
8/21/2008	59.26%	3.70%	25.93%	11.11%
8/22/2008	62.96%	7.41%	14.81%	14.81%
8/23/2008	38.89%	22.22%	22.22%	16.67%
8/24/2008	52.38%	19.05%	19.05%	9.52%
8/25/2008	52.17%	17.39%	4.35%	26.09%
8/26/2008	62.07%	6.90%	13.79%	17.24%
8/27/2008	71.05%	15.79%	5.26%	7.89%
8/28/2008	70.00%	0.00%	20.00%	10.00%
8/29/2008	65.38%	7.69%	7.69%	19.23%
8/30/2008	57.14%	14.29%	14.29%	14.29%
8/31/2008	43.33%	6.67%	36.67%	13.33%
9/1/2008	44.58%	4.82%	34.94%	15.66%
9/2/2008	59.50%	13.22%	13.22%	14.05%
9/3/2008	64.09%	16.57%	14.92%	4.42%
9/4/2008	64.05%	13.16%	11.14%	11.65%
9/5/2008	66.80%	15.81%	7.51%	9.88%
9/6/2008	57.55%	22.64%	10.38%	9.43%
9/7/2008	74.49%	10.20%	4.08%	11.22%
9/8/2008	67.07%	13.41%	4.88%	14.63%
9/9/2008	66.67%	13.33%	11.67%	8.33%
9/10/2008	65.06%	14.46%	8.43%	12.05%
9/11/2008	65.85%	17.07%	6.10%	10.98%
9/12/2008	66.18%	22.06%	4.41%	7.35%
9/13/2008	40.00%	26.67%	13.33%	20.00%

9/14/2008	67.57%	13.51%	10.81%	8.11%
9/15/2008	57.69%	15.38%	13.46%	13.46%
9/16/2008	60.61%	12.12%	21.21%	6.06%
9/17/2008	63.46%	9.62%	19.23%	7.69%
9/18/2008	55.88%	14.71%	11.76%	17.65%
9/19/2008	61.90%	11.90%	4.76%	21.43%
9/20/2008	58.82%	11.76%	14.71%	14.71%
9/21/2008	60.53%	2.63%	21.05%	15.79%
9/22/2008	72.34%	12.77%	8.51%	6.38%
9/23/2008	52.63%	15.79%	15.79%	15.79%
9/24/2008	66.67%	15.56%	11.11%	6.67%
9/25/2008	53.66%	9.76%	24.39%	12.20%
9/26/2008	67.57%	8.11%	16.22%	8.11%
9/27/2008	63.33%	16.67%	13.33%	6.67%
9/28/2008	48.00%	8.00%	20.00%	24.00%
9/29/2008	51.35%	24.32%	10.81%	13.51%
9/30/2008	58.00%	18.00%	16.00%	8.00%
10/1/2008	55.63%	11.27%	5.63%	27.46%
10/2/2008	59.20%	17.24%	9.77%	13.79%
10/3/2008	47.56%	23.17%	7.32%	21.95%
10/4/2008	68.66%	16.42%	8.96%	5.97%
10/5/2008	66.67%	15.69%	13.73%	3.92%
10/6/2008	59.21%	17.11%	13.16%	10.53%
10/7/2008	66.10%	13.56%	10.17%	10.17%
10/8/2008	57.50%	30.00%	7.50%	5.00%
10/9/2008	60.00%	12.73%	18.18%	9.09%
10/10/2008	63.64%	15.15%	18.18%	3.03%
10/11/2008	57.14%	21.43%	14.29%	7.14%
10/12/2008	68.89%	11.11%	15.56%	4.44%
10/13/2008	50.91%	12.73%	25.45%	10.91%
10/14/2008	66.67%	13.73%	11.76%	7.84%

10/15/2008	71.05%	10.53%	10.53%	7.89%
10/16/2008	57.58%	18.18%	12.12%	12.12%
10/17/2008	47.06%	26.47%	20.59%	5.88%
10/18/2008	74.19%	16.13%	9.68%	0.00%
10/19/2008	61.11%	13.89%	16.67%	8.33%
10/20/2008	46.67%	26.67%	20.00%	6.67%
10/21/2008	60.00%	15.56%	13.33%	11.11%
10/22/2008	56.41%	28.21%	7.69%	7.69%
10/23/2008	66.67%	8.33%	20.83%	4.17%
10/24/2008	51.52%	18.18%	18.18%	12.12%
10/25/2008	65.22%	17.39%	8.70%	8.70%
10/26/2008	60.00%	16.67%	20.00%	3.33%
10/27/2008	63.16%	18.42%	18.42%	0.00%
10/28/2008	60.00%	18.00%	18.00%	4.00%
10/29/2008	68.09%	21.28%	6.38%	4.26%
10/30/2008	72.97%	14.86%	6.76%	5.41%
10/31/2008	61.54%	15.38%	11.54%	11.54%
11/1/2008	48.98%	28.57%	2.04%	20.41%
11/2/2008	57.14%	15.87%	15.87%	11.11%
11/3/2008	73.03%	10.11%	11.24%	5.62%
11/4/2008	68.00%	16.00%	7.33%	8.67%

11/5/2008	63.51%	24.43%	5.17%	6.90%
11/6/2008	71.78%	14.11%	10.43%	3.68%
11/7/2008	70.00%	13.33%	7.78%	8.89%
11/8/2008	63.93%	21.31%	8.20%	6.56%
11/9/2008	70.00%	12.00%	10.00%	8.00%
11/10/2008	71.83%	9.86%	7.04%	11.27%
11/11/2008	63.89%	12.50%	15.28%	8.33%
11/12/2008	74.47%	8.51%	6.38%	10.64%
11/13/2008	66.13%	12.90%	8.06%	12.90%
11/14/2008	72.92%	8.33%	10.42%	8.33%
11/15/2008	55.81%	25.58%	6.98%	11.63%
11/16/2008	68.97%	6.90%	13.79%	10.34%
11/17/2008	66.67%	8.77%	7.02%	17.54%
11/18/2008	58.33%	18.75%	12.50%	10.42%
11/19/2008	69.39%	8.16%	12.24%	10.20%
11/20/2008	74.42%	6.98%	9.30%	9.30%
11/21/2008	59.26%	16.67%	5.56%	18.52%
11/22/2008	72.50%	2.50%	12.50%	12.50%
11/23/2008	57.89%	28.95%	5.26%	7.89%
11/24/2008	62.90%	12.90%	14.52%	9.68%
11/25/2008	65.85%	9.76%	4.88%	19.51%
	68.66%	11.94%	10.45%	8.96%

11/26/2008				
11/27/2008	66.04%	24.53%	5.66%	3.77%
11/28/2008	57.58%	24.24%	6.06%	12.12%
11/29/2008	68.42%	10.53%	15.79%	5.26%
11/30/2008	63.64%	9.09%	9.09%	18.18%
12/1/2008	53.65%	6.87%	30.90%	8.58%
12/2/2008	65.68%	13.27%	12.13%	8.92%
12/3/2008	68.13%	12.64%	10.99%	8.24%
12/4/2008	64.29%	15.00%	10.00%	10.71%
12/5/2008	62.22%	16.30%	11.85%	9.63%
12/6/2008	63.38%	8.45%	19.72%	8.45%
12/7/2008	67.11%	14.47%	7.89%	10.53%
12/8/2008	65.28%	9.72%	8.33%	16.67%
12/9/2008	64.41%	18.64%	3.39%	13.56%
12/10/2008	74.24%	9.09%	7.58%	9.09%
12/11/2008	71.43%	11.11%	4.76%	12.70%
12/12/2008	66.67%	14.29%	9.52%	9.52%
12/13/2008	61.22%	24.49%	4.08%	10.20%
12/14/2008	67.39%	17.39%	4.35%	10.87%
12/15/2008	61.19%	17.91%	1.49%	19.40%
12/16/2008	68.60%	13.95%	5.81%	11.63%
12/17/2008	69.35%	19.35%	4.84%	6.45%
12/18/2008	60.87%	8.70%	8.70%	21.74%
12/19/2008	54.17%	18.75%	10.42%	16.67%

12/20/2008	44.83%	37.93%	10.34%	6.90%
12/21/2008	50.00%	25.00%	8.33%	16.67%
12/22/2008	70.49%	9.84%	8.20%	11.48%
12/23/2008	63.64%	18.18%	6.82%	11.36%
12/24/2008	74.07%	14.81%	7.41%	3.70%
12/25/2008	61.90%	23.81%	9.52%	4.76%
12/26/2008	63.64%	12.12%	3.03%	21.21%
12/27/2008	39.53%	27.91%	9.30%	23.26%
12/28/2008	55.81%	11.63%	16.28%	16.28%
12/29/2008	46.51%	16.28%	29.07%	8.14%
12/30/2008	58.49%	13.21%	11.32%	16.98%
12/31/2008	59.46%	13.51%	16.22%	10.81%
1/1/2009	60.00%	6.88%	27.50%	5.63%
1/2/2009	62.50%	11.98%	15.36%	10.16%
1/3/2009	66.37%	10.76%	14.80%	8.07%
1/4/2009	63.64%	15.91%	12.50%	7.95%
1/5/2009	64.08%	17.14%	11.02%	7.76%
1/6/2009	53.72%	31.91%	5.85%	8.51%
1/7/2009	58.70%	23.91%	8.70%	8.70%
1/8/2009	66.25%	15.00%	12.50%	6.25%
1/9/2009	52.46%	29.51%	6.56%	11.48%
1/10/2009	48.28%	20.69%	17.24%	13.79%
1/11/2009	70.18%	8.77%	10.53%	10.53%
1/12/2009	68.42%	6.58%	13.16%	11.84%
1/13/2009	70.68%	11.28%	9.77%	8.27%

1/14/2009	69.62%	8.86%	7.59%	13.92%
1/15/2009	66.00%	14.00%	12.00%	8.00%
1/16/2009	54.90%	23.53%	3.92%	17.65%
1/17/2009	63.41%	12.20%	17.07%	7.32%
1/18/2009	73.91%	15.22%	8.70%	2.17%
1/19/2009	70.97%	6.45%	9.68%	12.90%
1/20/2009	72.41%	12.07%	3.45%	12.07%
1/21/2009	60.00%	20.00%	10.00%	10.00%
1/22/2009	66.22%	16.22%	8.11%	9.46%
1/23/2009	74.14%	8.62%	6.90%	10.34%
1/24/2009	57.14%	25.00%	14.29%	3.57%
1/25/2009	70.59%	7.84%	9.80%	11.76%
1/26/2009	75.00%	7.89%	6.58%	10.53%
1/27/2009	61.33%	13.33%	8.00%	17.33%
1/28/2009	66.15%	7.69%	10.77%	15.38%
1/29/2009	70.18%	10.53%	5.26%	14.04%
1/30/2009	64.29%	16.67%	2.38%	16.67%
1/31/2009	53.85%	25.64%	5.13%	15.38%
2/1/2009	59.04%	10.84%	20.48%	9.64%
2/2/2009	63.14%	8.33%	19.87%	8.65%
2/3/2009	69.32%	12.88%	11.36%	6.44%
2/4/2009	67.44%	13.37%	13.95%	5.23%
2/5/2009	65.35%	11.88%	9.90%	12.87%
2/6/2009	71.62%	10.81%	8.11%	9.46%
2/7/2009	68.33%	11.67%	10.00%	10.00%
2/8/2009	70.83%	4.17%	16.67%	8.33%
2/9/2009	66.67%	15.05%	8.60%	9.68%
2/10/2009	67.31%	5.77%	15.38%	11.54%

Accessed 11 February, 2009
(http://www.surveyware.com/report.aspx?qprid=1&qpnoauth=1&
qps=1&qpcustomc=99&qpcustom=595)

Data from Market Share: Top Operating System Share Trend

Accessed 11 February, 2009 from

http://marketshare.hitslink.com/os-market-share.aspx?qprid=9&qpdt=1&qpct=0&qptimeframe=M&qpsp=93&qpnp=24

I. Frequency Tables from Preliminary Survey

Respondent Gender

		Frequency	Percent
Valid	Undeclared	15	10.6
	Female	43	30.3
	Male	84	59.2
	Total	142	100.0

Sector

		Frequency	Percent
Valid	Public Sector	36	25.4
	Private Sector	63	44.4
	Public and Private Sectors	1	.7
	Total	100	70.4
Missing	System	42	29.6
Total		142	100.0

Industry

		Frequency	Percent
Valid	Undeclared	81	57.0
	Aviation	3	2.1
	Banking	3	2.1
	Charity	1	.7
	Educational	2	1.4
	Governmental	26	18.3
	Logistics	2	1.4
	Manufacturing	6	4.2
	Petroleum	9	6.3
	Press	2	1.4
	Real Estate	3	2.1
	Software	1	.7
	Telecommunications	3	2.1
	Total	142	100.0

Ease of using computers

		Frequency	Percent
Valid	Very Easy	78	54.9
	Easy	48	33.8
	Somewhat Difficult	11	7.7
	Difficult	5	3.5
	Total	142	100.0

Respondent Age (Binned)

		Frequency	Percent
Valid	18 - 21	14	9.9
	22 - 27	53	37.3
	28 - 33	31	21.8
	34 - 46	19	13.4
	Total	117	82.4
Missing	System	25	17.6
Total		142	100.0

Job

		Frequency	Percent
Valid	Undeclared	52	36.6
	Administrative	46	32.4
	Engineer	2	1.4
	Financial	3	2.1
	Human Resources	1	.7
	Labour	10	7.0
	Marketing	5	3.5
	Technical	23	16.2
	Total	142	100.0

Needs to Print

		Frequency	Percent
Valid	No	6	4.2
	Yes	136	95.8
	Total	142	100.0

Sends E-mail

		Frequency	Percent
Valid	No	7	4.9
	Yes	131	92.3
	Total	138	97.2
Missing	System	4	2.8
Total		142	100.0

Reads Arabic

		Frequency	Percent
Valid	No	24	16.9
	Yes	113	79.6
	Total	137	96.5
Missing	System	5	3.5
Total		142	100.0

Accesses Server

		Frequency	Percent
Valid	No	31	21.8
	Yes	79	55.6
	Total	110	77.5
Missing	System	32	22.5
Total		142	100.0

Reads PDF

		Frequency	Percent
Valid	No	20	14.1
	Yes	119	83.8
	Total	139	97.9
Missing	System	3	2.1
Total		142	100.0

Requires office Suite

		Frequency	Percent
Valid	Yes	32	22.5
Missing	System	110	77.5
Total		142	100.0

Uses Web Browser

		Frequency	Percent
Valid	No	11	7.7
	Yes	124	87.3
	Total	135	95.1
Missing	System	7	4.9
Total		142	100.0

Requires Spreadsheet

		Frequency	Percent
Valid	Yes	48	33.8
Missing	System	94	66.2
Total		142	100.0

Requires Word Processing

		Frequency	Percent
Valid	Yes	62	43.7
Missing	System	80	56.3
Total		142	100.0

Requires Presentation Software

		Frequency	Percent
Valid	Yes	26	18.3
Missing	System	116	81.7
Total		142	100.0

Requires Database

		Frequency	Percent
Valid	Yes	12	8.5
Missing	System	130	91.5
Total		142	100.0

Anti-Virus Installed

		Frequency	Percent
Valid	Yes	1	.7
Missing	System	141	99.3
Total		142	100.0

Uses HTML Editor

		Frequency	Percent
Valid	Yes	1	.7
Missing	System	141	99.3
Total		142	100.0

Needs Project Management Software

		Frequency	Percent
Valid	Yes	1	.7
Missing	System	141	99.3
Total		142	100.0

Plays Video

		Frequency	Percent
Valid	Yes	5	3.5
Missing	System	137	96.5
Total		142	100.0

Does Photo Editing

		Frequency	Percent
Valid	Yes	10	7.0
Missing	System	132	93.0
Total		142	100.0

Mail and Calendaring Application

		Frequency	Percent
Valid	Yes	27	19.0
Missing	System	115	81.0
Total		142	100.0

Logs into Active Directory

		Frequency	Percent
Valid	Yes	2	1.4
Missing	System	140	98.6
Total		142	100.0

Plays Real Audio and Video

		Frequency	Percent
Valid	Yes	5	3.5
Missing	System	137	96.5
Total		142	100.0

Uses Java Applications

		Frequency	Percent
Valid	Yes	4	2.8
Missing	System	138	97.2
Total		142	100.0

Edits Video

		Frequency	Percent
Valid	Yes	2	1.4
Missing	System	140	98.6
Total		142	100.0

Communicates via Text Chat

		Frequency	Percent
Valid	Yes	2	1.4
Missing	System	140	98.6
Total		142	100.0

Develops with Visual Basic

		Frequency	Percent
Valid	Yes	2	1.4
Missing	System	140	98.6
Total		142	100.0

Desktop Publishing

		Frequency	Percent
Valid	Yes	2	1.4
Missing	System	140	98.6
Total		142	100.0

Uses Exchange E-mail Service

		Frequency	Percent
Valid	Yes	1	.7
Missing	System	141	99.3
Total		142	100.0

SAP User

		Frequency	Percent
Valid	Yes	11	7.7
Missing	System	131	92.3
Total		142	100.0

Uses Lotus Notes Messaging

		Frequency	Percent
Valid	Yes	1	.7
Missing	System	141	99.3
Total		142	100.0

Compresses Files

		Frequency	Percent
Valid	Yes	2	1.4
Missing	System	140	98.6
Total		142	100.0

Needs Other Software

		Frequency	Percent
Valid	Yes	5	3.5
Missing	System	137	96.5
Total		142	100.0

AutoCAD User

		Frequency	Percent
Valid	Yes	3	2.1
Missing	System	139	97.9
Total		142	100.0

GIS System User

		Frequency	Percent
Valid	Yes	1	.7
Missing	System	141	99.3
Total		142	100.0

3DSMax User

		Frequency	Percent
Valid	Yes	1	.7
Missing	System	141	99.3
Total		142	100.0

Accesses an Oracle Database

		Frequency	Percent
Valid	Yes	1	.7
Missing	System	141	99.3
Total		142	100.0

J. Frequency Tables from Post-Experiment Survey

Subject Age (grouped)

		Frequency	Percent
Valid	18 - 22	7	13.5
	23 - 31	24	46.2
	32 - 39	9	17.3
	40 - 48	12	23.1
	Total	52	100.0

Subject Gender

		Frequency	Percent
Valid	Female	22	42.3
	Male	30	57.7
	Total	52	100.0

Job Specialization

		Frequency	Percent
Valid	Unemployed	7	13.5
	Academic	8	15.4
	Administrative	21	40.4
	Finance	3	5.8
	Financial	1	1.9
	Sales	1	1.9
	Technical	11	21.2
	Total	52	100.0

Computer Proficiency

		Frequency	Percent
Valid	Low Proficiency	8	15.4
	Medium Proficiency	33	63.5
	Expert Proficiency	11	21.2
	Total	52	100.0

Ease of Vista

		Frequency	Percent
Valid	Hard	5	9.6
	Easy	27	51.9
	Very Easy	20	38.5
	Total	52	100.0

Ease of Linux

		Frequency	Percent
Valid	Very Hard	1	1.9
	Hard	4	7.7
	Easy	26	50.0
	Very Easy	21	40.4
	Total	52	100.0

Satisfaction with Vista

		Frequency	Percent
Valid	Not Satisfied	3	5.8
	Almost Satisfied	11	21.2
	Satisfied	19	36.5
	Very Satisfied	19	00.5
	Total	52	100.0

Satisfaction with Linux

		Frequency	Percent
Valid	Not Satisfied	2	3.8
	Almost Satisfied	8	15.4
	Satisfied	25	48.1
	Very Satisfied	17	32.7
	Total	52	100.0

Agree to use Vista at work

		Frequency	Percent
Valid	No	17	32.7
	Yes	35	67.3
	Total	52	100.0

Agree to use Linux at work

		Frequency	Percent
Valid	No	19	36.5
	Yes	33	63.5
	Total	52	100.0

Preferred solution at work

		Frequency	Percent
Valid	Neither	1	1.9
	Linux	23	44.2
	Vista	28	53.8
	Total	52	100.0

Made in the USA
Lexington, KY
14 October 2010